THE FOUR FACES OF GOD

**A Different Perspective on the Sudden Appearance
and Evolution of Humankind**

*For my good friends Joseph
and Gwen*

Laurence Bergeron

Laurence Bergeron

Printed in the United States of America.

Book Design and Editing by Professional Publications

The Four Faces of God

"Their faces looked like this: Each of the four had the face of a man, and on the right side each had the face of a lion, and on the left the face of an ox; each also had the face of an eagle"

Ezekiel 1:10

"In the center, around the throne, were four living creatures, and they were covered with eyes, in front and in back. The first living creature was like a lion, the second was like an ox, the third had a face like a man, the fourth was like a flying eagle"

Revelation 4:6

DEDICATED TO JUDITH DEMERTGIS

TABLE OF CONTENTS

THE FOUR FACES OF GOD

ACKNOWLEDGMENTS

I would like to thank all of my friends and family who supported and encouraged me throughout the lengthy research and writing of this book. Special thanks go to my editor, Carol Ann Johnson, not only for her invaluable assistance, but also for her patience and understanding through dozens of rewrites and minor changes in the original manuscript. I would also like to thank her for help with the original cover design. Although this book carries my name, and I alone am responsible for its content, it would never have been written without the support and help from all of the people who have traveled down this long path with me.

THE FOUR FACES OF GOD

PREFACE

Recently, in the Altai Mountains of Siberia, a fossil finger bone was discovered that DNA paleontologists claim belongs to a previously unknown species of man that lived at least 30,000 ago. Because of the huge distance from the African cradle of modern man, this species clearly must have traveled over a vast area, and yet its existence has remained hidden until now. Given this, how many other species of human beings may be out there yet to be discovered?

THE FOUR FACES OF GOD

FOREWORD

It has always amazed me that, although no one alive today was witness to the event and stories were written by unknown authors nearly sixty years after, millions of people throughout the world are convinced beyond a shadow of a doubt that Jesus not only rose from the dead, but that it was proof that he was the divine son of God. At the same time, despite thousands of reliable eyewitness accounts and hundreds of photographs, video tapes, and radar records, most of these same people are openly skeptical of the existence of interplanetary spacecraft piloted by extraterrestrial beings visiting earth. Most believe, unquestionably, that God exists, although there is not a shred of credible evidence to confirm this belief. I have often wondered what a man would believe if he were not subject to years of indoctrination into contemporary religious dogma from the very beginning of his intellectual being.

When one is a young child, adults have all the answers; they even know why the sky is blue. Illogical mythical characters such as Santa Claus are accepted, for a while, because their existence has been confirmed by a mutually accepted adult conspiracy to hoodwink their young. Even older siblings, once on to the game, join in to perpetuate the joke on those too young to understand. While this is harmless fun, God is serious business.

God must be real since everyone, or at least it seems everyone, believes it. The Bible must be the word of God, Jesus must be God's only begotten son, and there must be a heaven and a hell. We are made in God's image. He loves us and wants us to be free of sin. Life is the entrance exam to heaven. All these things must be true. Why else would we as a people invest so much into building churches and expend so much time in prayer. After all, isn't the national motto "In God we trust"? When so many believe, how can it not be true?

This book is not about God. It is more about religion than about God. But, it is fundamentally about man's inability to reason when the conclusions of logic run against the grain of religious faith, even if the religious faith is not his own. When it comes to religion, man faces the ultimate test of peer pressure. Not only does the non-believer face the wrath of the majority, but he also risks banishment to the bowels of the hell by a vengeful God.

This book is about what I believe, not because this is what I have been taught, but because this is what seems logical to me. Predictably, there will be critics and religious zealots that will call this sacrilegious nonsense or, worse still, total nonsense. It is not my intention to attempt to prove that my ideas are correct. It is my intention to encourage one to think beyond what he can see in front of his face today and what he will wear to work tomorrow. It is in fact, theory and conjecture, but it is no less theory and conjecture than

Catholicism or Buddhism when placed under the microscope of close scrutiny. It is about the mystery of the origins of humankind. It is about life's possibilities, about setting aside entrenched preconceived notions of reality, about setting aside, some of those things you were taught in biology class and all of those things you were taught in Bible school. To quote Clarence Darrow's observation about the existence vis-à-vis the non-existence of God: "I do not pretend to know, where many ignorant men are sure."

THE FOUR FACES OF GOD

CHAPTER 1 - IN THE BEGINNING

Starting about sixty thousand years ago, a genuine mystery occurred. In a cosmic nanosecond, modern man, Homo sapiens sapiens, appeared out of Africa and began populating the planet Earth. Thirty thousand years later, all other species of Homo, including the robust Neanderthal that had survived for 250,000 years, had become extinct.

In 1925, this country witnessed what was then called the "trial of the century" when a Tennessee high school teacher, John Scopes, was convicted of violating a state law against teaching the theory of evolution in the classroom. Some eighty years later, the issue of evolution versus creationism (the notion that the origin of the world, and man himself, was literally, as the book of Genesis describes) is still being contested. There is today an undercurrent of sentiment, which is attempting to place evolution into the category of an alternate theory to creationism rather than an undisputable scientific fact. In the fall of 2004, the school board in Dover, Pa became the first in the country to require teaching "intelligent design" – a euphemism for creationism – as an alternative to evolution in high school biology. The argument for intelligent design hinges on the missing transitional fossils that would link ancient forms to their contemporary ancestors. The intricate complexity of life is only possible, they argue, if intelligent design (God) has a hand in creating

1

it. While this may not be true for life itself, there may be some reason to suspect a helping hand in the design of man.

Evolution is an excruciatingly slow process. Although the earth was formed approximately 4.6 billion years ago, life did not originate until 1 billion years later. Somewhere between 3.8 and 3.5 billion years ago the first organisms, prokaryotes or bacteria, appeared. No other life forms existed on Earth for the next billion years. The first multi-celled animals did not appear until about 600 million years ago. 150 million years later, we have the first fish (it wasn't until 375 million years ago that fish finally moved onto land.) 140 million years after the first fish, the first reptiles appear, and after another 85 million years, (about 225 million years ago), the first mammals. Mammals, however, made little evolutionary progress until 65 million years ago when the dominant life form, the dinosaurs, were wiped out by the catastrophic aftermath of a collision between the Earth and a large meteorite. With their king-sized competitors gone, small mammals began to develop rapidly, increasing in both variety and size.

Still, the origins of modern mammals go back millions of years. Apes first appeared around 23 million years ago, the giraffe 30 million years ago, and the ancestors of the horse can be traced back 55 million years. The common ancestor of man and chimpanzee, our closest genetic family member, is believed to have lived between 6 and 8 million years ago. To put this whole evolution thing into proper perspective, if the entire history of the Earth is considered to be a one-year period, this common simian ancestor of man would have shown up about 13 hours before midnight on December 31. Modern man himself has been around for just the last 7 minutes. In other words, modern man's portion of this one-year symbolic representation of time is 411 seconds out of a total of 31,536,000 seconds.

When we finally arrived, in the last half of the last day of the Earth's cosmic year of history, evolutionary progress, at first, was slow. One of man's earliest ancestors, Australopithecus, changed very little in the 2.5 million year time span of their existence. They essentially reproduced and avoided extinction. Then, some extraordinary evolutionary events began to occur. About two million years ago, the Homo group appeared. This included the subspecies Homo habilis, Homo rudolfensis, and Homo erectus. Although both Austrapihecus and the Homo species were bipedal and walked upright, Homo's legs were longer, his arms were shorter, and his jaw and teeth were different. The difference in the male and female size was 15% compared to a difference of 50% for Austrapihecus. Most significant of all, however, the brains of both H. rudolfensis and H. erectus were almost twice as large (800 cc compared to 450 cc) as the Austrapihecus. This was the most rapid increase in brain size in man's history or the history of any animal for that matter. The interesting thing is that the Homo group does not appear to be descended from any know species of Austrapihecus, although it is believed that both originated in

Africa. Homo is thought to have evolved from some unknown Austrapihecus species, although this "missing link" – nor any of these missing transitional fossils - has ever been discovered.

After this extraordinary evolutionary spurt, Homo erectus, the most successful of the homo species, changes very little during the next million years with the exception of a further (but slower) increase in brain size to a capacity of 1000cc. In the process, H. erectus had spread from Africa into Asia and Europe. Somewhere around 500,000 years ago, Homo erectus split into two groups leading eventually to Homo sapiens and Neanderthal. Homo sapiens appear to have originated from the African group while the Neanderthals trace their linage to the European branch. This Asian branch would later mysteriously disappear. Neanderthals flourished in Europe and the Near East from 250,000 to 30,000 years ago, after which, they too would mysteriously disappear. Homo sapiens appeared about 200,000 years ago and subsequently spread throughout the world. It wasn't until about 60,000 years ago, however, that modern man—Homo sapiens, sapiens[1]—the new improved version of Homo sapiens with an even larger brain capacity

---

[1] Sapiens, a Latin word meaning "wise." Homo sapiens, the species Latin name of Human beings. (ergo, the wise, wise man) Retrieved from http://en.wikipedia.org/wiki/Sapiens. (n.d.) Wikipedia The Free Encyclopedia.

of 1350 cc, leaves Africa and spreads throughout the planet. All other Homo species, including the Neanderthals, vanish into the fossil records.

What is wrong with this picture? If things had progressed according to the laws of natural selection, the Neanderthal should still be around. Neanderthals had begun evolving in Europe perhaps 500,000 years ago, later spreading throughout all of Europe, the Near East and Central Asia. This species was much more powerfully built than modern man, and had a brain capacity that was actually larger (1600cc versus man's 1350cc). Because they were thickly built, they were well suited to cold climates. They made tools that included stone knives and spears and were skillful hunters of large mammals such as deer and bison. Yet, despite their superior size, strength and adaptation to cold weather, the Neanderthal was somehow surpassed by modern man who migrated out of a warm African climate into a cold Europe in the middle of the last Ice Age. The consensus appears to be that they were "out competed" for resources by the more technologically advanced newcomers. At one time it was thought that Neanderthal and modern man may have interbred, but recent DNA studies have shown that this was not the case; albeit there are "trace" amounts of Neanderthal DNA in modern man's DNA suggesting that there may have been "incidental contact." Neanderthal DNA is unique and doesn't belong with either modern man or ape. Not only does this place them in a role as an entirely different species, although with a common ancestor to man; it also

5

confirms that there was no detectable admixture[2]. According to geneticist Spencer Wells, all humans living today can trace their Y-chromosomes back to a modern man, actually a woman, living in Africa some 60,000 years ago. Neanderthal was both a genetic and evolutionary dead end. However, the question remains; how could relatively weak, hairless, smaller brained modern man replace within an evolutionary blink of an eye his physically stronger, cousin who had managed to adapt and survive for more than a quarter of a million years? It runs completely contrary to the laws of natural selection.

Evolution through natural selection involves the accumulation of small random mutations in both plants and animals, which, quite by accident, help them adapt to changes in their environment. Those better adapted to the change are most likely to survive and pass on these advantages to succeeding generations. A simple example of this would be that the coats of brown rabbits would gradually change to white as they migrated to the Artic. Lighter colored rabbits, would be harder for predators to spot, and would be more likely to survive. Over hundreds of generations, this would result in exclusively white rabbits in the Artic snow. The

---

[2] The result of interbreeding between two or more previously isolated populations within a species. Retrieved from http://en.wikipedia.org/wiki/Admixture. n.d. Wikipedia The Free Encyclopedia.

same principle applies to the predators such as foxes, wolves and bears. Most predators and prey have coats that provide camouflage in order to hide from each other. The same type of animal may have many different types of coats depending on its environment. Lions match the golden grass of the African plains, while leopards match the shadows on the jungle floor.

Other factors can also play a role. Climate changes, for example. If the climate gets drier, those plants and animals that can make the best use of limited water survive. Thus, we get the cactus and the camel. Certain kinds of animals do better in different climates. More heat, more reptiles, less heat, fewer reptiles. Colder climates beget better fur coats. And so it goes. The basic premise is that in static conditions, the strongest survives and in changing conditions, the most adaptive survive. However, the key element is that evolutionary adaptation is an extremely slow process. These changes do not occur overnight. Even a rather simple genetic shift requires thousands of generations for a beneficial mutation to occur. Let me repeat that these changes happen over hundreds or thousands, or even hundreds of thousands, of years. Natural selection it is a result of purely random adaptation to slowly changing conditions. Lucky chance or mutation can spell the difference between survival and extinction of a species. But the general rule prevails, evolution moves ever so slowly.

Selective breeding, on the other hand, is a very rapid, deliberate process. Since man first began domesticating animals some 10,000 - 15,000 years ago, we have bred thousands of different breeds, often with specific purposes in mind. We have hunting dogs and sheep dogs, milk cows and meat cows, and turkeys that grow too fat to fly. Bad attributes can be bred out, while good attributes can be bred in. Do you want white rabbits? It is no problem simply to breed the white ones. New breeds of white rabbits or of "pure-bred" dogs can be realized within only a few generations. Genetic engineering makes our cattle fatter, our corn sweeter, and our pumpkins larger. Beginning in 1959 at the Institute of Cytology and Genetics in Novosibirsk, Siberia, researchers were able genetically to domesticate wild foxes through selective breeding within only a dozen generations. Miraculously, they had compressed thousands of years "natural" domestication into just a few years. Today these genetically engineered foxes are as tame as your household cat or dog.

Researchers are currently working on a new way to kill cancerous tumors using genetically engineered viruses that replicate only in cancer cells and subsequently destroy them, leaving the healthy cells untouched.

Humankind is on the verge of its greatest advancement since the industrial revolution. With planned genetic engineering, we can make people healthier, smarter, stronger and free from disease. By tinkering with their genes, scientists have already engineered worms that live six times their normal life span. Although humans are much more complex than worms, within this century, it may well be that we will find a way to slow the aging of our cellular machine and postpone old age for decades. In the not too distant future, we may be "growing" new limbs and organs from patient's stem cells. But, of course, we don't do that; at least, not yet.

To summarize; we have the first "human" about eight million years ago. About two million years ago, we make a major leap to a human animal with several distinct changes, the most important of which is the dramatic increase in brain size. Afterwards, there is nothing new until the split of Homo sapiens and Neanderthal species from a common ancestor around 500,000 years ago. 250,000 years later, the Neanderthal becomes the dominant species in Europe and the Near East, while Homo sapiens spread from Africa into all other parts of the world. Finally, about 50,000 years ago, modern man, Homo sapiens sapiens, appear in Africa and within the next 30,000 years or so, spread throughout the earth and apparently contribute to the demise of both his Homo sapien and Neanderthal cousins. It is interesting to note that while Neanderthals held their own against Homo sapiens, they seem to have met their match with the new and only slightly different Homo sapiens sapiens.

It didn't take long before the new improved version of man got down to the business of civilization building. Modern man begins settling into villages, planting crops, and breeding farm animals around the end of the last Ice Age - approximately 13,000 years ago. Then things begin to pick up speed. Around 3500 BC, three separate advanced civilizations appeared simultaneously in the same general area of the Earth. One was the Indus on the Indus River in India; one was the Mesopotamia on the Euphrates River in what is now Iraq; and one was the much more familiar Egyptian civilization on the Nile River. Suddenly, we have gone from living in mud huts in the jungle to constructing complex cities with huge stone buildings. This is not so much a genetic miracle as it is a cultural evolutionary one, but it is still remarkable and mysterious none-the-less.

Even if we start counting at about two million years ago, the great preponderance of man's existence has been spent hunting for dinner and finding a warm place to sleep. Only in the last .0065% of our time on Earth have we done anything constructive. What caused us to shift gears? After all, we had been doing ok for the last few million years. Why start building cities all of a sudden? And, it was all of a sudden.

Most animals have just enough brain to get by. Crocodiles still make do with the same size brain they had 65 million years ago. Even our close relatives, the great apes, are probably no more intelligent than they were a one or two million years ago. What is it that has caused the human brain to expand so dramatically in the past two million years? Traditional theory contends that after man came down out of the trees, due to a changing African climate, escape from predators became more difficult, thus forcing a dependence on ingenuity. This may explain the changes that occurred one million years ago. But what about the subsequent jumps in brain capacity? Why after a slow increase in Homo erectus' brain size over one million years is there a sudden spurt from 700cc to 1000cc in late Homo erectus, culminating with the increase to 1600cc for the Neanderthal some 250,000 years ago? The tendency of natural selection is to drift towards the norm, i.e. brain size, once sufficient for basic survival it should tend to stabilize. Why didn't brain development plateau at about 700cc, which seems to have been easily enough to survive?

This is exactly what appears to have happened to one recently discovered "lost" branch of the Homo erectus tree. In November 2004, a team of Australian and Indonesian Scientists announced that they had discovered remains of 3 ft. tall humanoids dubbed Homo floresiensis, which may have co-existed with modern man as late as 13,000 years ago. Although not a close relative, they did evolve from our common ancestor Homo erectus. What is remarkable about these small humans is that their brains were only about the size of a grapefruit – smaller than a chimpanzee. Despite their small brains, however, they were smart enough to use fire, make tools, and hunt. If we could do all this with these small brains, what was it that suddenly propelled modern man's brain to its current size?

In addition, why did homo's teeth, especially the molars, become smaller over time? Why are we so physically scrawny? A gorilla is three times larger but eight times stronger than a man and the gorilla never visits the gym. The chimpanzee is twice as strong as man. How did we become so weak? However, the most intriguing mystery of all is what happened to man's fur coat? Most mammals have fur coats. Monkeys have fur coats, gorillas have fur coats, and our closest biological relative, the chimpanzee has a fur coat. Why don't we? Yes, we seem to have a remnant of a fur coat – some of us more than others – but compared to most mammals we are pretty much sans hair. Although I recently read someone's theory that we are hairless because our prehistoric ancestors found hairlessness sexy, the generally accepted theory seems to be that once we started wearing clothing we lost our need for fur coats. This begs the question, however, as to why we started wearing clothing in the first place.

CHAPTER 2 - PROJECT EARTH

Humans and chimps share 99.4 percent of their DNA, the molecular code for life. In fact, chimps and humans share a common ancestor that lived about 7 million years ago. We are more closely related to chimps than chimps are to gorillas. One study published in May 2006 in *Nature* indicated that the human-chimp speciation was very unusual in that it may have happened in two stages, the first some 10 million years ago when humans and chimpanzees first split up. Then, after evolving in different directions for about 4 million years, they briefly got back together for a brief fling that produced a third, hybrid population with characteristics of both lines. That genetic collaboration resulted in two separate branches – one leading to humans and the other to chimps some 6 million years ago. Admittedly, this seems very strange and has inspired skepticism in many paleontologists; but, whatever the case, comparisons of the human genetic code's 3.1 billion DNA letters and those of the chimpanzee confirm long-held suspicions that we differ by only about 1 percent. According to Morris Goodman at Wayne State University of Medicine, "we humans appear as only slightly remodeled chimpanzee-like apes." He would classify both humans and chimps in the same genus Homo. In the seven million years since the split from our common ancestor, we seem to have fared much better on the development road than our cousin the chimp. The .6 percent of DNA that we don't share accounts for a heck of a lot of difference, including it seems, our lack of a fur coat. But, more importantly, we have a huge brain that provides for our ability for abstract thought, a spoken language, and an overwhelming propensity to build and create. Why didn't the chimp develop these attributes? If we started out with the same ancestor, why are we now so smart, and the chimp so relatively stupid? They had as much evolutionary time as we did. Some of the difference must have been evolutionary, but that cannot account for such a wide discrepancy in only six or seven million years.

In March 2004, a team of biologists and plastic surgeons at the University of Pennsylvania reported in the journal Nature their theory that a mutation – a gene that led to smaller weaker jaws and, ultimately, bigger brains – accounts for the development that separated man from apes. Their contention was that smaller jaws would have fundamentally changed the structure of the skull by eliminating thick muscles that worked like bungee cords to anchor a huge jaw to the crown of the head. The change would have allowed the cranium to grow larger resulting in the development of a bigger brain capable of tool making and language. Their estimate of when this mutation occurred was about 2.4 million years ago in the grasslands of East Africa, a period in time that coincides with the first fossils of prehistoric man featuring rounder skulls, flatter faces, and smaller teeth and jaws. Non-human primates, including the chimpanzee, still carry the larger, more powerful jaw gene and the smaller, less powerful brain. Interestingly, since about two million years ago, the human brain has nearly tripled in size.

This report was immediately attacked by other scientists with one declaring it "counter to the fundamentals of evolution." Other researchers disagreed that human evolution could literally hinge on a single mutation of the jaw muscles. So far, perhaps 250 genetic differences have been identified between humans and chimpanzees pointing to the conclusion that many additional mutations are probably needed to explain all the changes seen in the human fossil record.

Even 250 genetic changes in the past 2 million years appear, to me, to be contrary to the "fundamentals of evolution." The crocodile is much the same as he was one hundred million years ago. Despite the dinosaur's two hundred million years or so of genetic opportunity, they never did get around to so much as basic tool making. Why didn't they? They certainly had plenty of time. Why didn't the poor chimp get his share of those 250 genetic changes, or at least enough of them to enjoy daytime TV? Conversely, why aren't we still scratching around in the forest looking for something to eat?

The logical answer is that man could not be where he is today without the help of some form of deliberate biological genetic engineering. Obviously, this could only come from a species beyond our current level of technological development, albeit only slightly above. After all, the human

15

race has been, genetically engineering domestic animals and crops for thousands of years; and we are, even now, routinely cloning animals, which will inevitably include humans. We are on the verge of using genetic engineering to grow new limbs and organs, and to wipe out and/or cure many diseases, which have a genetic base. I will bet, if we really tried, we could, in the not-too-distant future, genetically engineer our own "super chimp" to do more important things than serve as medical research lab specimens and space capsule test drivers. But whose "super chimps" are we?

Could it be that humankind is nothing more than some galactic biology project? Could it be that aliens from distant parts of our galaxy have been genetically altering humans for the past two million years? Wouldn't that possibility answer all the questions about the sudden rapid increase in brain size, the decrease in the size of jaw and teeth, the missing body hair, the small muscles, and even the male baldness gene? Is this where we got our creative inclinations, our ability for abstract thought, and our moral sense of right and wrong? Could this also explain the huge volume of "unused" brain cells and the physic abilities of a very few "gifted" individuals? Could these physic abilities that we find so rare be traces of alien traits that are common to them, but have not quite been transferred to us? Could the Neanderthals have been one test project that didn't quite measure up? Could modern man be a subsequent test project that turned out to be an "improved model" – a relative success? Is it possible that the mysterious disappearance of the

Neanderthal and all other species of Homo after the appearance of modern man were the result of some ethnic cleansing by the aliens to insure the success of their latest and greatest model? Perhaps they used a virus or some sort or sterility radiation to eliminate their old projects. This would explain the sudden demise of the Neanderthal and all of our other genetic cousins. Imagine how devastating a virus such as HIV could be to a population without modern medicine. What saved man from such horrendous diseases in the distant past have been the mountain ranges between the tribes. This would have only been a small technicality for beings possessing flying machines and hypodermic needles. Remember, to them, this is just a science project. Their concern would compare to ours should we have a plague killing off all the rabbits in Australia.

This alien science project would also explain the wide range of intelligence in humans. Despite an average IQ of 100, the human IQ bell curve runs in a wide range of from 50 to 180. Natural selection over eons of time should push IQ towards a mediocre average, which, by the way, is what appears to be happening today. But, where do the IQ anomalies, the edges of the bell curve, come from and why does the right side of the bell curve, the smart side, extend so much further than the left?

Let's assume that the original sample homo animal, as a result of natural selection, had an IQ of 50 (just enough for basic survival) before alien genetic engineering. Let's also assume that they used their genetic code to cross breed and that the alien average IQ was in the 300-400 range. We should logically get a hybrid human animal with an IQ of around 200 plus. If the aliens created enough of these IQ superstars, they could infuse an intelligent quotient injection into the entire human race. In the beginning, however, these superstars would have become the "god-kings" of developing ancient civilizations and they were probably segregated from the "lowly" masses. The aliens were the gods and the superstar humans were the god-kings. Thus perhaps begins the tradition of divine rulers that has existed for thousands of years.

The problem is that, after the aliens depart, the human IQ becomes watered down through interbreeding with the non-superstars and the original civilization decays into a less advanced state. The good news, however, is that although the average IQ slopes down from the super star level, it never quite slopes back down to the original level of 50 – it levels off at, let us say, 100, which has always been considered "the norm." Actually, recent studies haves shown the average IQ is now about 96. Which proves to me, at least, that the average IQ is still in the process of being "watered down." The less intelligent humans have become more prone to reproduction (or conversely, there appears to be a decline in the propensity to procreate among the better educated who recognize the correlation between children and wealth).

Actually, in 2002, the average IQ in the United States was estimated to be 98 according to a controversial book by Dr. Richard Lynn, Professor Emeritus of Psychology at the University of Ulster, Northern Ireland, and Dr. Richard Lynn, Professor Emeritus of Tamper, Finland. According to Wikipedia, the book argues that differences in national income (in the form of per capita gross domestic product) correlate with differences in National intelligence quotient (IQ). The authors have established an estimated value of 82 countries and the average IQ ranges from a high of 107 in Hong Kong to a low of 59 in Equatorial Guinea.[3]

Be that as it may, the resultant drop in IQ over time has had little effect on our ability to survive since the average human IQ was already in excess of what is needed for basic survival; but it does affect the ability of human kind to develop unilaterally. In fact, the "survival" of humans possessing lower than average IQs is supported by those having above average IQs in that they provide artificial intelligence, "instruments of convenience," for the less gifted (i.e. the computer). Civilization never slips back to the cave dwelling tribal IQ level, but continues, instead, with its downward "intellectual drift." Initially the overall average IQ of the general population would go up from 50 to 100 or

---

[3] For those who are interested, the results of their study, including the complete list of 82 countries with corresponding IQs can be found on the internet at Wikipedia, the free encyclopedia under "IQ and the Wealth of Nations."

higher, maintaining civilized structures and eventually, in the end, would give us the capacity to find and use technology. A strange by-product is that every so often we have the throw back to the alien created super-stars. We get a Michelangelo, a Leonardo da Vince, a Newton, or an Einstein. We get that occasional genetic bounce into the upper level of the IQ curve. This could be our leftover alien DNA heritage. Along these lines, one might also argue that when we get the occasional moron, this could be a throwback to our original human heritage. In fact, it appears as if much of our original heritage still exists and is driving on our highways.

IQ enhancement projects would probably have spanned the entire two million years, not gradually, as in the natural evolutionary process, but with quick periodic injections, beginning with the first Homo species and more or less ending (here on Earth, at least) as recently as 10,000 years ago. Since then, it appears that our alien fore fathers have been busy working on our cultural development elsewhere.

That we are of this planet earth is a virtual certainty based on our 99.4% of chimpanzee DNA; but it might very well be that the other .6% is, at least, in part composed of DNA provided courtesy of alien genetic engineers in search of an improved earth creature that was closer to their own level of intelligence. It may have been that they needed human labor more accustomed to earth's air and/or gravity or it may have simply been their purpose to roam through the universe seeding intelligence into appropriate candidates. Their "five year mission" was to explore new worlds and seek out new beings that only need a little shot of intelligence in order to join the upper ranks of the galactic community. Perhaps that will be **OUR** mission someday. The scary thought is that maybe Morris Goodman was more correct than he knew when he said, "We humans appear as only slightly remodeled chimpanzee-like apes." We may, in fact be merely slightly remodeled versions of the chimpanzee itself. It is somewhat humbling to contemplate, but our chimp cousins may just be the ones who didn't get the DNA injections.

Why didn't our alien creators just set up their own housekeeping on Earth instead of screwing around with us for the past two million years? Perhaps they were just passing through the galactic neighborhood and stopped to plant a few genetic seeds before moving on. Perhaps they didn't like the weather and the insects just as some dislike Florida for the same reasons. Maybe the oxygen levels were too high or too low for them. Maybe our sun was too strong. Maybe they didn't eat meat and their food wouldn't grow here. On the other hand, perhaps they did stay. Perhaps they have been coming and going for eons; and perhaps they are still here. . .

Does all of this sound a little far-fetched – even a little crazy? Well, the evidence is all around us. It is found in all the ancient records that survive to this day. Let us begin with the record most Americans are familiar with – The Bible.

CHAPTER 3 - THE WRITTEN RECORD

"So God created man in his own image, in the image of God he created him; male and female he created them." Genesis 1: 27[4]

Why in God's image? God, in the traditional spiritual sense, would have no physical image. In whose image were we created then? Could it be someone or something that looks (or thinks) somewhat like we do now, but with a little more compassion and a lot less violence?

"When men began to increase in number on the earth and daughters were born to them, the sons of God saw that the daughters of men were beautiful and they married any of them they chose." Genesis 6:2

". . . when the sons of God went to the daughters of men and had children by them. They were the heroes of old, men of renown." Genesis 6:4

Sons of God and daughters of men; why this separate distinction? The products of these relationships were "heroes of old and men of renown." What made them so special?

---

[4] Unless otherwise noted, most references to the Bible throughout this work are from the New International Version copyright 1986 by Zondervan Publishing House

"The Lord appeared to Abram and said, "To your offspring I will give this land." Genesis 12:7

"The Lord said to Abram after Lot had parted from him, "Lift up your eyes from where you are and look north and south, east and west. All the land that you see I will give to you and your offspring forever." Genesis 13:14 & 15

After the appearance of Noah, God is referred to in the Bible as "the Lord" and He appears to be very much involved in the day-to-day business of Abram. He seems to be acting in the above passages as some sort of generous landowner. Later, the Lord becomes interested in the activities of Abram's wife Sarai's maidservant Hagar, who is also Abram's pregnant mistress. Abram, at the time, is eighty-five years of age. I am not making this stuff up. Perhaps because she is only a maidservant (and a little bit of a slut to boot) the Lord doesn't personally go to speak with Hagar when she runs away because Sarai has been mistreating her. He sends an "angel" instead – one of the Bibles first, but certainly not last, reference to these mysterious messengers. After asking Hagar just where the hell she thinks she is going . . . .

'The angel added 'I will so increase your descendants that they will be too numerous to count.'" Genesis 16:10

This is a promise that both The Lord and God seem to hand out liberally.

"The angel of the Lord also said to her: 'You are now with child and you will have a son. You shall name him Ishmael . . .'" Genesis 16:11

Predicting pregnancies and the sex of the child before the advent of ultra-sound seems to have been a particular skill of angels in the Bible well into the New Testament.

"But the angel said unto him, Fear not, Zacharias for thy prayer is heard; and thy wife Elisabeth shall bear thee a son, and thou shalt call his name John." Luke 1:13

"And the angel said unto her, Fear not, Mary, for thou hast found favour with God. And behold thou shalt conceive in thy womb and bring forth a son, and shalt call his name JESUS." Luke 1: 30-31

This would not be as impressive a trick if the angels were orchestrating the conception as artificial insemination or "immaculate conception." In Genesis 17, when Abram is ninety-nine (and just getting started) the Lord tells him that "I am God almighty" and the Lord is referred to as God again for the rest of the chapter. But God is just as interested in Abram's business and his reproductive affairs as the Lord was.

In this chapter, God establishes a "covenant" with Abram and his descendants. However, this is pretty much a one-way deal as God sets all of the terms and conditions, one of which is that Abram and his wife Sarai shall change their names to

Abraham and Sarah respectively. The term "shall" is used to this day in United States Government contracts to define what the contractor shall do as opposed to what the Government will do. Then God tells one hundred year old Abraham that his ninety-year old wife Sarah is going to have a son that he will call Isaac. God, (and his angels) it seems, also likes to pick out the baby's name to go along with the prediction.

Later, in Chapter18, the Lord is back, but this time in the form of three strangers who also have the ability to make the same prediction to Abraham, although who is doing the talking (the Lord or these three men) is unclear. What is particularly interesting about this passage is that the three strangers have the ability to read Sarah's thoughts, much like that of aliens described in UFO abduction stories. After this, at least two of these men, later referred to as angels, head off down the road to help the Lord destroy Sodom and Gomorrah.

The destruction of the city of Sodom and Gomorrah is an interesting side note. Supposedly, this city was destroyed by God because of the decadence of its populace.

"Then the Lord said, 'The outcry against Sodom and Gomorrah is so great and their sin so grievous . . .'" Genesis 18:20

The next few passages lead one to believe that the Lord is destroying this city because of the wicked ways and sexual perversions of its inhabitants. If this is the case, folks in cities from New York City to Los Angeles had better start thinking about packing their bags and getting out of town. Why would the Lord destroy Sodom and Gomorrah for what amounts to a little sexual excess, while overlooking more serious offensives in the future such as the multiple genocides throughout history (some of which continue today in Africa) and the "holocaust" of WW II? If there was a city of Sodom and Gomorrah and if the Lord destroyed it, you can bet that he did so because its inhabitants had done something against "the rules"; i.e. his rules; i.e. the alien rules. Sodom and Gomorrah more than likely was used as an example, as a warning to others to "toe the line." You must bear in mind that these are English translations from the Greek translations from whatever and these final translations were done by Christian Monks who would very likely put their own (sex is sinful) slant on it. In any case, if the message was "perverse sex is bad" some folks just didn't get the message. Shortly after the Lord destroys Sodom and Gomorrah with what looks to be very much like an atomic weapon—"the smoke of the country went up as the smoke of furnace" (Genesis 19:28)—the two daughters of Abraham get him drunk and have incestuous sex with him (Genesis 19:32). Apparently, the Lord lets this slight indiscretion slide since there are no resultant divine repercussions. I suppose sin is judged according to scale.

Now that you have the general idea, it should be sufficient to say that throughout the remainder of Genesis,

God, the Lord, and the Lord's angels stay very much involved in the family affairs of Abraham and his descendants. Further special attention is given to reproduction – something like a cross between Peyton Place and Father Knows Best but in much more detail than one needs or wants to know about. God displays a good deal of pettiness, issuing orders and smiting all those "who trespass against him" or otherwise don't see things quite his way. God appears to have had an enormous amount of free time on his hands during those days for conversing with mere mortals judging by the number and the length of such conversations contained therein.

Exodus is much of the same except that God is now concerned with the affairs of the Egyptians in general and of Moses in particular. Before Moses meets God for the first time, during which time they engage in another lengthy conversation, Moses sees "an angel of the Lord" in a "burning bush"- a story that is familiar to every Sunday school attendee. When Moses goes over to inspect the mysterious "burning" bush that does not burn, God warns him not to come any closer. The bush is safe, but maybe not Moses.

Then he says, "I am the God of your father, the God of Abraham, the God of Isaac and the God of Jacob." Exodus 3:6

"And," he may as well have added, "I am going to be your God also, by God" because from this point forward, Moses is directed by God to go forth and do this and go hither and do that. As early as Genesis 12, there are references to both

28

Egypt and the Pharaoh, and the Bible begins to replace pure legend with some historical material. Although it is hard to tell exactly what Egyptian period is floating in the background, Moses is believed to have been born around 1300 BC. So we can place all of God's historically busiest (at least the best documented) interference in mankind's affairs 2000 years after the time we were getting those brand new civilizations off the ground. But, I digress.

Every Christian child is familiar with the Ten Commandments given to Moses, but even before God has finished helping Moses liberate the Israelites from Egypt in Exodus 12:5, he is issuing directives right down to what and when to eat. However, he did step in with a huge assist with his considerable hi-tech powers when needed. Though it has been noted many times before, it is still interesting to note again in this book that upon leaving the land of Egypt, the Israelites were guided by what appears to be some sort of flying craft.

"By day, the Lord went ahead of them in a pillar of cloud to guide them on their way and by night in a pillar of fire to give them light." Exodus 13:21

Later when the Pharaoh and his chariots are closing in on the fleeing Israelites, this mysterious craft moves around to separate the two and protect the latter.

"Then the angel of God, who had been traveling in front of Israel's army, withdrew and went behind them. The pillar of cloud also moved from in front of and stood behind them. . ." Exodus 14:19

Even in the last line of the last chapter of Exodus, that strange cloud is still hanging around.

"So the cloud of the Lord was over the tabernacle by day and fire was in the cloud by night, in the sight of all the house of Israel during all their travels." Exodus 40:38

Once the Egyptians have been dispatched and the Israelites are "safely" in the desert, God begins to preach and lay down the law with great gusto. Beginning with the Ten Commandments in Exodus 20, God spells out in infinitesimal detail, instructions and laws concerning the treatment of servants, personal injuries, protection of property, social responsibility, justice and mercy, and the Sabbath. In this regard, it is interesting to compare the following:

"But if there is serious injury, you are to take life for life, eye for eye, tooth for tooth, hand for hand, foot for foot, burn for burn, wound for wound, bruise for bruise.

"If a man hits a manservant or maidservant in the eye and destroys it, he must let the servant go free to compensate for the eye." Exodus 21:23 - 26

"If a man destroys the eye of another man, they will destroy his eye. If he breaks the bone of another man, they will break his bone. If he destroys the eye of a subordinate or breaks the bone of a subordinate, he shall pay one mina of silver." From the Law Code of Hammurabi given to King Hammurabi of Babylon from Shamash the Sun-God and Patron of Justice, c. 1750 BC.

Neither the God of Moses nor the sun god of King Hammurabi appears to be a proponent of equal opportunity (or equal treatment in this case). It doesn't seem quite God-like justice from either one, but, at least, they are consistent. So, the next time you use the familiar quote "an eye for an eye" you should include "unless it is the eye of a servant" if you wish to be technically accurate.

The book of Leviticus continues this extensive catalogue of detailed instructions including the burnt offering, the grain offering, the fellowship offering, the sin offering, the guilt offering, eating fat and blood (forbidden), clean and unclean food, purification after childbirth, regulations about infectious skin disease, regulations about mildew, unlawful sexual relations, and punishment for sins (adultery was a capital offense). In fact, the entire book is a compilation of rules and regulations that would make any government proud.

What does all this prove? It proves nothing. But, what it suggests is that God, the Lord, and angel(s) of the Lord are interchangeable manifestations of the same being and that this being or beings, although similar in appearance to man, processes extraordinary God-like powers that are freely wielded to both reward and punish. Most importantly, it suggests that these beings are extremely interested in our

31

behavior, our morals, and our reproduction. Between the lines, however, one can read that at this point in our history (somewhere around 1300 BC) these beings are losing, or have lost, control of the majority of mankind and are concentrating their efforts on small groups or individual families while attempting to get some written legal and moral fundamentals established. The writings of Old Testament appear to have originated at the end of the Alien golden era when they were much more in control of things. After 2000 BC, the aliens appear to begin to use human ambassadors to spread their gospel and keep their finger in our collective pie.

Perhaps you are one of those so secure in your faith that you would prefer to believe that God actually materialized from "heaven" in some sort of human appearance and engaged in extensive conversations with, among others, Abraham and Moses about what actually amounts to a mountain of mundane things in the galactic scheme of things. I mean, shouldn't God have been off creating new worlds or something? God certainly doesn't appear to have spent much time talking with the Pharaoh or the Egyptians, possibly because they were worshipping idols and such, but a divine prejudicial slight non-the-less. At least, the Egyptians didn't record any divine sightings. What they did record was sightings of "strange lights in the sky." When you think about it, does the idea that it was alien beings doing all of this interference in our affairs sound any more far-fetched than the idea of God taking time out in 1300 BC to become involved in man's affairs? If it were God, in the traditional

Christian sense, he appears to have packed his bags and moved on by the time of Jesus. With the exception of a reference to the Spirit of God descending like a dove" and "a voice from heaven" (Matthew 3:17), the New Testament contains no such descriptions of discussions, or even sightings, of the Lord, albeit the "angels of the Lord" appear to still have been around. Today, we have apparently been completely abandoned since we have no recent sightings of either God or his angels. What we have sighted recently, however, in extremely large numbers, has been mysterious lights in the sky, alien craft and alien beings. Not surprisingly, these strange craft described are in the biblical record in places other than Exodus. One of the best is that contained in Ezekiel 1.

CHAPTER 4 - THE PROPHET EZEKIEL, DANIEL AND THE SHINY ONE

"In the thirtieth year, in the fourth month on the fifth day, while I was among the exiles by the Kebar River, the heavens were opened and I saw visions of God . . .

I looked and I saw a windstorm coming out of the north – an immense cloud with flashing lightning and surrounded by brilliant light. The center of the fire looked like glowing metal, and in the fire was what looked like four living creatures. In appearance their form was that of a man, but each of them had four faces and four wings. Their legs were straight; their feet were like those of those of a calf and gleamed like burnished bronze. Under their wings on their four sides they had the hands of a man. All four of them had faces and wings . . ." Ezekiel 1:1-8

What is clear from this passage is that Ezekiel has seen some sort of shining flying craft that is especially bright. What is not clear is whether the four creatures he describes are part of this flying machine, robots, or men in metallic-like suits, helmets, and shiny boots. The wings could be anything.

"Their faces looked like this: Each of the four had the face of a man, and on the right side each had the face of a lion and on the left the face of an ox; each also had the face of an eagle." Ezekiel 1:10

Most modern interpretations of Ezekiel 1 skip over this part, but this is a most intriguing passage. Are these just mechanical similes or do they represent painted symbols on the machine or on helmets of the creatures? Animals play a big part in the ancient Egyptian religious life – there was even a cult that worshipped the bull. The huge sphinx in Egypt is a man's head on the body of a lion. Both the lion and the eagle have been extensively used as national symbols. In fact, the eagle is a part of the Great Seal of the United States. Is this all just a coincidence or is this a carryover of symbolism from days gone by?

"The appearance of the living creatures was like burning coals of fire or like torches. Fire moved back and forth among the creatures; it was bright and lightning flashed out of it. The creatures sped back and forth like flashes of lightning." Ezekiel 1:13-14

Although Ezekiel specifies that it is the fifth day of the fourth month, he doesn't say whether it is day or night, but this sounds very much like flashing lights, strobe lights, or both.

"As I looked at the living creatures, I saw a wheel on the ground beside each creature with its four faces. This was the appearance and structure of the wheels: They sparkled like chrysolite, and all four looked alike. Each appeared to be made like a wheel intersecting a wheel. As they moved, they would go in any one of the four directions the creatures faced; the wheels did not turn about (or aside) as the creatures went. Their rims were high and awesome, and all four rims were full of eyes all around.

When the living creatures moved; the wheels beside them moved; and when the living creatures rose from the ground, the wheels also rose. Whenever the spirit would go, they would go, and the wheels would rise along with them, because the spirit of the living creatures was in the wheels. When the creatures moved, they also moved; when the creatures stood still, they also stood still; and when the creatures rose from the ground, the wheels rose along with them, because the spirit of the living creatures was in the wheels." Ezekiel 1:13-21

Whatever else he was not, Ezekiel was certainly precise. Unfortunately, this paragraph is as unclear as it is precise. He could be describing four parts of the machine or four similar machines. The "eyes" may or may not be portholes. The only thing that we are sure about from this passage is that whatever the wheels were, they were mechanical, they were round and they made a big impression on Ezekiel. But, if you were a primitive person, how would you describe your first encounter with a brightly lit, noisy, flying piece of machinery?

"Spread out above the heads of the living creatures was what looked like an expanse sparkling like ice, and awesome. Under the expanse their wings were stretched out one toward the other, and each had two wings covering its body. When the creatures moved, I heard the sound of their wings, like the roar of rushing waters, like the voice of the Almighty, like the tumult of an army. When they stood still, they lowered their wings." Ezekiel 1:22- 24

Could the "expanse sparkling like ice" be a Plexiglas bubble cockpit? Could the wings be rotor blades? Could the "roar of the rushing waters" be the sound of an engine?

"Then there came a voice from above the expanse over their heads as they stood with lowered wings. Above the expanse over their heads was what looked like a throne of sapphire, and high above on the throne was a figure like that of a man. I saw that from what appeared to be his waist up he looked like glowing metal, as if full of fire, and that from there down he looked like fire; and brilliant light surround him. Like the appearance of a rainbow in the clouds on a rainy day, so was the radiance around him.

This was the appearance of the likeness of the Lord. When I saw it, I fell face down, and I heard the voice speaking." Ezekiel 1:25-28

Here we have what appears to be a man in an extremely shiny suit sitting on a metal seat in a cockpit illuminated by bright electric lights. Obviously, the lights and the suit are designed to make an impression on Ezekiel and the rest of the natives. Wouldn't we feel the same?

"He said to me, 'Son of man, stand up on your feet and I will speak to you.'" Ezekiel 2:1

You can bet that he is using a loudspeaker device to further enhance the impression of power. This is apparently a recruitment mission for a messenger of God since this God-like creature goes on to lay out a list of go-hither-and-do instructions for Ezekiel and gave him something to eat that "tasted as sweet as honey in my mouth". Then the Lord takes him for a ride in flying machine.

"Then the Spirit lifted me up, and I heard behind me a loud rumbling sound – May the glory of the Lord be praised in his dwelling place! - the sound of the wings brushing against each other and the sound of the wheels beside them, a loud rumbling sound. The Spirit then lifted me up and took me away . . ." Ezekiel 3:12-14

Mission accomplished! Ezekiel is whisked away to be with the exiles that lived at Tel Abib, ". . . And there, where they were living, I sat among them for seven days – overwhelmed." Ezekiel 3:15

After this, Ezekiel is put through some sort of training program where he receives instruction from the Lord on everything from soup to nuts and usually beginning with the phrase "The word of the Lord came to me." Moreover, the Lord usually refers to Ezekiel as the "son of man." Some of this dialogue is very charming, including "very well" he (the Lord) said, "'I will let you bake your bread over cow manure instead of human excrement.'" Ezekiel 4:15

And, the shiny one shows up again in Ezekiel 8.

39

"In the sixth year, in the sixth month on the fifth day, while I was sitting in my house and the elders of Judah were sitting upon me, the hand of the Sovereign Lord came upon me there. I looked, and I saw a figure like that of a man. From what appeared to be his waist down he was like fire, and from there up his appearance was as bright as glowing metal. He stretched out what looked like a hand and took me by the hair of my head. The Spirit lifted me up between earth and heaven and in visions of God he took me to Jerusalem." Ezekiel 8:1-3

Ezekiel never fails to be impressed.

Of course, you could choose to believe that what Ezekiel really saw was God riding in a chariot of fire and light and pulled by four angels. On the other hand, you could dismiss the whole passage as total nonsense; whatever makes the most sense to you.

But whether God or alien, he must have had a fast motorcycle because the shiny one shows up again in Daniel 10.

"On the twenty-fourth day of the first month, as I was standing on the bank of the great river, the Tigris, I looked up and there before me was a man dressed in linen, with a belt of the finest gold around his waist. His body was like chrysolite, his face like lightning, his eyes like flaming torches, his arms and legs like the gleam of burnished bronze and his voice like the sound of a multitude." Daniel 10:4-6.

Coincidently, the South American "Jesus" known by the ancient Indian people of the Andes as "Viracocha", a tall white, bearded man who wielded extraordinary power, shared a knowledge of science and magic, and healed the sick by touch, was assisted, according to legend, by beings known as "the shiny ones" (hayhuaypanti).

Daniel also had visions of four strange animal-like creatures that "came up out of the sea."

"'The first was like a lion, and it had the wings of an eagle.'" Daniel 7:4

A second beast looked like a bear and the third looked like a leopard, but the leopard has on its back "four wings like those of a bird" and "this beast had four heads." Daniel 7:6

The fourth beast, however, is the strangest of all "terrifying and frightening and very powerful. It had large iron teeth; it crushed and devoured its victims and trampled underfoot whatever was left. It was different from all the former beasts, and it had ten horns." Daniel 7:7

Could this have been some sort of armored vehicle or vehicles; or was this just a dream? Moreover, why does the number four continue to come up over and over again?

CHAPTER 5 - THE ARCHEOLOGICAL RECORD

Planet earth is littered with alien postcards. Throughout the modern world are mysterious ancient souvenirs from our past; structures and objects made from stone of whose age we can only guess. Included in these are the Pyramids and the sphinx of Giza. In the case of the Great Pyramid of Khufu, what is particularly astonishing is the mathematical precision of the construction.

The Great Pyramid of Khufu, the largest at Giza, is thought to have been built around 2550 BC during the reign of the Pharaoh Khufu in the Egyptian Fourth Dynasty- some 4500 years ago. Covering more than 13 acres and rising to a height of 481 feet, the Great Pyramid contains 2.3 million blocks of limestone and granite weighing between 2 and 70 tons apiece. It rests on a limestone platform that is level to within 7/8 of an inch and is precisely aligned to the four points of the compass. The difference between the longest side at the base and the shortest side is less than 8 inches out of a total average length per side of 9063 inches – an error amounting to only a fraction of one percent – and the corners, while not perfect, are extremely close to being exactly 90 degrees. This in a structure weighing 6 million tons and containing more stone than all the cathedrals, churches and chapels built in England since the time of Christ. At forty stories, it was the tallest structure in the world until 1889 when the Eiffel Tower was constructed to a height of 984 ft.

Deep within the heart of this great pyramid is the so-called "Kings Chamber." This room is 19 feet 1 inch in height and has a perfect 2:1 ratio dimension of 34 feet 4 inches long by 17 feet 2 inches wide. It is situated approximately 150 feet high within the pyramid itself and is precisely oriented east and west (long side) by north and south (short side). The sides of the room are composed of 100 granite blocks weighing 70 tons each and the roof is capped with nine additional stones of 50 tons each. To put this in perspective, each seventy ton block is equal to the weight of thirty-five large automobiles and is five tons heavier than America's heaviest armored vehicle; the 65 ton Abrams M1A1 tank. Building this room, therefore, is the equivalent of lifting 100 of these huge tanks 150 feet into the air and arranging them into a perfect 2:1 rectangle. The logistics of doing this, even today, is staggering. Contemporary theory is that these huge blocks were pulled up ramps (across logs serving as wheels) by hundreds of workers. Modern railroad standards for a 6,000 horsepower locomotive pulling an appropriate load of cars specify not more than a three percent grade: that is, an incline that goes up 3 feet vertical for every 100 feet of horizontal travel. Increases of even 1 or 2 percent of this require additional locomotives as steeper grades require exponentially more power to overcome the gravitational pull. There arrives a point wherein the slope of the grade requires an incredible amount of force to overcome gravity. If the

Egyptians used a maximum theoretical grade of nine percent, the length of a ramp necessary to attain 150 feet would be almost a mile long and contain more material than the pyramid itself. In addition, this doesn't address the problem of moving these 70-ton monsters into place once on top of the grade nor the placement of nine 50-ton blocks located above the walls, one atop the other, with "compression" spaces between. Keep in mind that much of the 6 million tons of stone remains above this room.

Originally, the three pyramids at Giza were covered with a mantel of polished limestone blocks so carefully joined that it was impossible to see the joint from more than a few feet away. The angle of the combined slope of these stones on the Pyramid of Khufu and hence the pyramid itself, was 51 degrees 51 minutes. Why this strange angle? As it turns out, the angle of the slope determines the height of the structure. This angle was apparently deliberately chosen to set the height of the great pyramid at precisely 481.3949 feet, which, when multiplied by two and divided into the combined length of the four sides at the base of 3023.14 feet, equals 3.14. This is remarkably close to the value of pi; a mathematical relation to the perimeter of its base to the radius of a circle is to its circumference. The value of pi was not "rediscovered" until the sixth century AD. Remarkably, this same factor of pi is built into the Pyramid of the Sun at Teotihuacan in Mexico in a relationship of four times the height divided into the sum of the sides at the base. More than just the shape of the Egyptian and Mayan pyramids connects these two monuments. They are linked by a shared demonstration of this primary geometric equation that shines out to us like a beacon.

More intriguing still is the so-called sarcophagus enclosed within the walls of the Kings Chamber. Thought to be the tomb of Khufu, it is carved from a single piece of chocolate colored granite and is too large to have been carried through the entrance corridor. Once again, we find a mathematical signpost. The external volume (outside dimensions) of the sarcophagus is precisely twice that of the internal volume (inside dimensions). This precision was achieved deliberately. The sarcophagus stone was cut from its surrounding granite block to a measurement of 7 feet 5.62 inches long by 3 feet 2.5 inches wide and 3 feet 2.5 inches deep. After which this huge, incredibly hard stone was hollowed out to an interior measurement of 6 feet 6.6 inches long, 2 feet 2.81 inches wide, and 2 feet 2.81 inches deep. We are supposed to believe that this work was cut to machine age tolerances by ancient Egyptians using bronze tools. It is thought that only circular drills using cutting jewel points could have cut out the inside of the stone, but no such tools have ever been found by Egyptologists.

There are other mathematical messages incorporated into the Kings Chamber. The height of the room is exactly one half that of the floor diagonal. The dimensions of the room can be dissected in such a way as to arrive at the "golden section" value of phi, which is the square root of 5 plus 1 divided by 2 or 1.61803 – another one of those strange numbers, like pi, that can be carried out to decimal point infinity. Other mathematical clues built into the Great Pyramid suggest whoever built it also knew the precise circumference of the Earth, the exact length of the calendar year, and the distance to the sun. How could the Egyptians possibly have known that last one?

Why do we see all this mathematical science and precision in what Egyptologists claim was merely a tomb for the Pharaoh Khufu? If it is a royal tomb, why are there no hieroglyphs on the walls within the pyramid as there are in all the "confirmed" tombs of the pharaohs? Most tombs of the pharaohs were extensively decorated. None of the passageways of any of the pyramids have any inscriptions or decorations what so ever, although there are some graffiti and "quarry marks" of dubious origin found behind the stones of the "relieving chambers" above the Kings Chamber. Supposedly discovered by Colonel Howard Vyse in 1837, these hieroglyphic writings that include references to Khufu are cited by Egyptologists as proof positive that the Great Pyramid was built by Egyptian workers for the Pharaoh Khufu. There is, however, some archaeological evidence that the Great Pyramid was already in existence long before Khufu came to the throne, but Egyptologists have chosen to ignore this.

There are other questions. Why would the time line for tombs for the Pharaohs proceed from immense pyramids to caves in the Valley of the Kings? Shouldn't it have been the other way around? Could it be that the dozens of crumbling, imperfect pyramids scattered about Egypt are failed copies of the much older original pyramids rather than crude first attempts as the Egyptologists claim? Who can say for certain which rock is the older? I have read, but can no longer locate the reference, that Greek historians wrote that the Great Pyramids existed long before the Egyptian empire and were as mysterious to them as they are to us today.

Even if you assume that the Great Pyramid was built as a tomb, why would any ruler or any people devote so much time and national treasure to making something so difficult to build with such precision, when so many other more useful, less precise, things could have been achieved with much less money and effort (money counted, even then)? What kind of mindset and power must one wield to convince primitive, ill-equipped people to move millions of tons of stone into a technically worthless, yet still perfectly formed, monument? It only makes sense if it had another purpose and, in fact, wasn't all that difficult to do. Egyptologists estimate that it took 100,000 men 20 years to build the pyramids. How could these still primitive people have done this?

It is far more likely that these three pyramids at Giza were designed and built in a matter of a few days by computerized machinery that included laser "saws" and anti-gravitational lifting devices that cut and carried the huge stones from the quarry, all under the direction of our alien forefathers, via a master designer computer. Interestingly, only the largest pyramid (Khufu) has the magnificent mathematical precision. The other two pyramids appear to be built simply to show those who would later find these structures the exact celestial origin of those that built them.

In 1993, an amateur astronomer, Robert Bauval, noticed that an aerial view of the three pyramids of Giza matched up perfectly in size, orientation, and relative distance apart to the three stars in Orion's belt. Moreover, after further investigation, it appeared that the Giza structures taken in whole, amounted to a land based picture of the Orion constellation, not as they appeared from Earth in 2500 BC, but as they appeared in 10,450 BC. There are also indications of water erosion damage on the great lion/man statue of the Sphinx, thought to be a contemporary structure of the Giza pyramids. There has been no significant rainfall in this area since before 10,000 BC. Could it be that the Sphinx was built long before the Egyptian empire, possibly long before 10,000 BC, and could it be that the original head was that of a lion, later altered by the Egyptians ("face of a lion") or was the headdress of the head of the man/lion copied by the Egyptians? Could it be that the Great Pyramid was built at a time when the aliens first arrived and were at the top of their game as a form of cosmic graffiti as if to say, "We were here, we are from the Orion system, and we are magnificent"? Was this an alien equivalent of the American flag on the moon? Perhaps the Great Pyramid had originally been painted with the four faces, one of each face on each of the four sides. It may have only been only later that the aliens help develop the Egyptian civilization.

In the ninth century AD, the Muslim Governor of Cairo, Caliph Al-Ma'mun, instructed a large team of men to tunnel into the Great Pyramid based on ancient rumors that there were hidden chambers inside that held, not only the Pharaoh's gold, but also magical things such as "metal that would not rust and glass that would not break." As their good fortune would have it, just prior to giving up, they accidentally broke into the main passageway that descended from a hidden entrance that they had searched for but could not originally find. Following this passageway, they came upon an ascending passageway, but this was blocked by huge granite plugs that they could neither break through nor dislodge. Unable to break through, Ma'mun's men tunneled around them through the softer limestone. Obviously, they thought, as we would, that they must be the first ones to enter into whatever lay beyond; at the very least a chamber full of treasure, if not magical things. What they eventually found was a chamber (the "king's chamber") that contained nothing, nada; with the exception of the empty lidless chocolate colored granite sarcophagus. Although a ridge along the top suggest that there was once a lid, no lid has ever been found.

The smaller chamber, the so called "queens chamber," that is located further down was also completely empty. Why would anyone go through all the trouble of building this enormous structure and then seal it up empty? That makes no sense what so ever. Yet, how could anyone else have gotten there first and stolen the contents? Even in ransacked tombs, the thieves usually leave something seemingly worthless behind. This so-called tomb was as clean as a hounds tooth. There is speculation by some that this tomb was robbed by the end of the Old Kingdom in 2150 BC, but, if so, how did the robbers get in and out, and what did they do with the sarcophagus lid? Why would they take it even if they could? If the first part of the puzzle is when, how, and why was it built, the second part has to be what ever happened to what was in there, if there was anything there at all?

Could the Great Pyramid been some sort of historic marker/time capsule that was intended to encapsulate scientific knowledge for later, smarter, more advanced generations of mankind to unravel and use? Did the aliens change their minds and steal their own scientific secrets back through another yet to be discovered secret passage or even through the stone itself? Perhaps they thought we would never measure up, that we would always be too violent, too out of control, and lacking sufficient altruism. Could this be when man tasted the fruit (or stole some fruit) from the forbidden tree of knowledge and was thrown out of the Garden of Eden? Are there hidden chambers still full of alien promise and alien answers in the Pyramids or the Sphinx yet to be found by yet more modern technology? Only time will tell.

Another possibility, and I stress possibility, is that encased within some inaccessible chamber of the Great Pyramid (or all three of the Pyramids for that matter) may reside a galactic homing beacon beaming a signal to any alien craft arriving from any constellation facing the northern hemisphere. The huge mass of the Pyramid would protect both the transmitter and the power source from any damage and would be designed to last for eons. The Pyramid complex may have been the epicenter of a large alien base. Is the fact that it is located in Africa, the land from which all species of man, and in particular, Homo sapiens sapiens, originated a coincidence, or is there a connection? Other stone ruins have been discovered off the relatively shallow waters of both Japan and Bimini in the Bahamas. These underwater structures must have been constructed prior to 10,000 BC before the sea level would rise to bury them. During the last Ice Age peak, about 20,000 years ago, the sea level would have been 400 feet lower than it is today. 20,000 years ago is roughly the same time that modern man was spreading out and settling across the planet. In-as-much-as the Earth revolves, there may have been "navigation homing beacons" in several areas of the Earth including Japan and the Bahamas. Could it be that the old (now underwater) beacon in the Bahamas is responsible for the examples of erratic compass and aircraft instruments reported in this area. I myself have experienced a rapidly spinning magnetic compass on a boat in Bahamian waters for no apparent reason while the GPS remained stable.

Originally, and for quite some time, archaeologists have believed that modern humans first crossed into North America via an ice bridge across the Bering Strait from Asia about 12,000 years ago, near the end of the Ice Age. Recently, this theory has been challenged by the discovery of some evidence that modern man was, in fact, in the North American continent much earlier, possibly even as early as 50,000 years ago. This long-range estimate is based on measures of radioactive carbon traces found in remains of plants alongside human artifacts, including flint blades and tool chips, found in a hillside along the Savannah River in Georgia.

Other recent evidence from sites in Chile and Oklahoma has suggested modern man may have inhabited the Americas as far back as 30,000 years ago. There are skeletal remains that indicate that modern man had already populated Southeast Asia and Australia 50,000 years ago. Out of Africa and into the Americas and Australia within 10,000 years is spectacular. To put this into perspective, Neanderthal man never got beyond Europe or the Near East in the 250,000 years of their existence. Unlike the Neanderthal, modern man was obviously not content simply to sit around the campfire talking about the tomorrow's big woolly mammoth hunt. They were on the move. Where did this spark come from?

Another strange occurrence is, that in the relatively few short years they were populating the planet, modern man appears to have broken apart into several different distinct races. If modern man originated out of Africa, why isn't the only race on Earth the Negro race? How did man evolve so many different physical differences in such a short time? Could this possibly have been a random event in such a short period, or were refinements still being made on the final human product?

Recently, some of the oldest artworks ever found, figurines carved from mammoth ivory, were discovered in a cave in Germany. Radiocarbon dating used to date the carvings are imprecise, but the objects were almost certainly made between 28,000 and 35,000 years ago. The carved figurines include a water bird, what appears to be a horse's head, and a lion-man. The one-inch lion-man is similar to a nearly foot-long figurine previously found in a nearby valley. These are believed to be the work of modern man rather than the contemporary Neanderthal who lived in the same area around this time. What is interesting to note, at least to the author, is that we have, 30,000 years ago and thousands of years before Ezekiel, a carved depiction of three of the "four faces of God." All that we are lacking, although some readers may disagree, is the bull.

Between 20,000 and 10,000 years ago, many strange things appear to happen, although most of these occurred closer to the 10K than the 20K period. These events include:

1. the population of all the major continents (except Antarctica) by modern man,

2. the mysterious disappearance of Neanderthal,

3. the first appearance of works of art (although the small bird figurine made from mammoth ivory discovered in Germany dates back 30,000 years),

4. the first ocean going watercraft,

5. the first domestication of animals,

6. the first appearance of agriculture,

7. the construction of what are now underwater stone structures,

8. and, very possibly the construction of the Great Pyramids and the Sphinx.

Surely, man could not be doing all this construction while he was at the same time traveling, unless, of course, he was getting help with both the construction and the traveling.

Could this have been the period in which the alien's cosmic biology project was peaking, when they were calling all the shots and everything was going according to their game plan? They had rid the planet of genetic experimental failures and had spread their new "super ape" across the entire planet. Is this the time of the mythical Atlantis and/or the mythical Garden of Eden? Was our collective hand being held and our future being molded by our alien makers?

This is a photograph of the stones at the lowest level of the Great Pyramid at Giza. The limestone rock is pitted by erosion by there is no appearance of anything similar to chisel marks.

1. The Great Pyramid at Giza in Egypt

Also, note the joint in the two stones in the foreground. It is irregular, yet the stones fit together like two pieces of a jigsaw puzzle. How can this have been achieved? It almost appears as if the two stones have been "melted" together. Keep in mind that there are an estimated 2.2 million of these huge stones. If one assumes that these stones were cut and fitted by hand and if you were to calculate that it would take, conservatively, 400 man-hours to complete each stone, the total effort required to complete the entire pyramid would have been about 880,000,000 man-hours. How could this huge expenditure of labor have been used for this purpose when the early civilizations, like those today, needed more practical things, such as roads, canals and homes?

CHAPTER 6 - MYSTERIES OF A LESSER KIND

There are other ancient architectural mysteries, albeit less impressive in size and with less mathematical precision than the Great Pyramid. For example, we do not know the answers to the questions hiding behind the huge stones of Stonehenge. We do not know how they were cut, transported, and set up in their peculiar circle arrangement on a field in England. They appeared supposedly around 2950 BC, but may have been much earlier. Even if we accept the date of construction as 2950 BC (about 5000 years ago), the key question here as with the Pyramids, is why? Why would ancient people who must be "just getting by" in primitive conditions do this? Logic dictates that these folks should have been using their energy looking for a meal and a warm place to sleep rather than moving 35 ton pieces of stone over 20 miles for some sort of community project (try getting a few of your neighbors together for this kind of fun).

The involvement of aliens in this instance is less likely, or, at least, less pervasive, since the project lacks the perfection and the "in your face" majesty of the Great Pyramid. Still, you have to question why these ancient people at a basic subsistence level of existence in a harsh land with a not so great climate would expend valuable energy moving around these multi-ton stones for "mystical" reasons, not to mention how they managed to accomplish it. This one is so strange that I don't even want to go there.

57

An amazing discovery in southeastern Turkey is currently getting close scrutiny years after its original discovery by a Turkish Farmer in 1960. At a site named Göbekli Tepe — the Turkish name for "pot-bellied hill"— a huge prehistoric site is being excavated, which pre-dates anything found to date. Thought to have been built about 11,500 years ago, predating the pyramids by a staggering 7000 years, these ruins include carved and polished circles of stone that feature huge pillars of carved stone, some of which weigh 19 tons and stand 17 feet tall. At least 50 of these huge pillars have so far been uncovered.

A stone city of this size and complexity at such an early time in history is redefining everything previously thought about the beginnings of civilization. It reverses standard theories of the chronology of human origins, eliminating the old model in which men slowly evolved 10 to 12 thousand years ago through a gradual transition from farmers and shepherds to villages with specialized labor, writing, art, government, and organized religion. It appears now that, at some places in the world, civilization had reached an advanced stage at least 5000 years before previously thought.

Another mystery that I have not a clue about, yet intrigues me still, is the existence of ancient, almost perfect stone spheres, found in Costa Rica measuring up to 6 feet in diameter, but with radial accuracy within 0.07 inches. How and why could these be constructed using tools of the period? For what could they have been used? No one knows and I will not venture to speculate here. My only comment is that to make such a perfect sphere out of stone, for whatever the reason, could certainly not have been possible with the native technology then available.

Numerous pyramid shaped structures are scattered about what is now Mexico and Central America. These remnants of the Aztec and Mayan civilizations, while built in similar form to the Egyptian pyramids, were constructed differently, essentially using facing stone to cover fill material in the core as opposed to the solid stone construction of the Giza complex. Another difference was that the Central American people preferred their pyramids with steps, often on all four sides. Because they lack the huge 50-ton stones of other ancient structures, it is easier to accept that these buildings were constructed by man without any special wizardry or alien assistance, although the overall quality of the stonework is impressive.

What they did have in common with the Egyptian pyramids, however, was the alignment to the cardinal points of the compass and the preoccupation with mathematical and astrological symbolism. The Mayan pyramid at Chichen Itza located in the central Yucatan peninsula of Mexico, for example, has rather steep stairways on all four sides. Each contains 364 steps, that when taken together with the top platform equate to the 365 days of the solar year. This temple is precisely positioned in such a way that at the vernal and autumnal equinoxes special light and shadow effects create the allusion of a giant serpent undulating on the northern staircase. Nearby are ruins containing dozens, if not hundreds, of stone columns, both round and square, that at one time must have held up an enormous roof of unknown material. These columns are not unlike those used in ancient Egypt, Greece and Rome, except they lack the internal central connecting pegs used in the construction of the Greek columns.

50 kilometers northeast of Mexico City lay the ruins of the enormous ancient city of Teotihuacan. No one knows exactly when this city was built although estimates range anywhere from between 100 BC to 4000 BC. Nor do we know who built it, but it was laid out according to geometric design and, at its peak, contained thousands of buildings, 600 temples, and 200,000 people. It also contains a number of impressive structures including two pyramids – the larger known as that of the Sun and the smaller that of the Moon. The Pyramid of the moon is less than half the size of the Pyramid of the Sun, but still contains approximately one million tons of stone and earth. The two Pyramids combined contain approximately three and one half tons of material. This is little more than half of the six million tons of rock contained in the Great Pyramid, but it represents an extensive investment in manpower non-the-less. The base of the Pyramid of the Sun is slightly smaller than the Great Pyramid and the slope of its sides of 43.5 degrees (as opposed to 52 degrees for the Giza Pyramid) give it a lower

height of 233.5 feet. Since it is proportioned differently, the height x 2pi = perimeter of the base that works for the Great Pyramid does not work for the Pyramid of the Sun. However, its height (233.5 feet) x 4pi does equal the perimeter of its base (2932.76 feet). This strange angle of slope of 43.5 degrees, rather than an easier to calculate 45 degrees must have been, as in the case of the Great Pyramid, done deliberately to incorporate the value of pi into the ratios of the building. Why would they do this other than to make a statement, as did the builders of the Great Pyramid? They wanted us to know clearly that they were aware of this unique value.

In the mountains above the Urubamba Valley in Peru at an elevation of 7,710 feet above sea level is a well-preserved pre-Colombian Inca ruin known as Machu Picchu. Unlike other Inca ruins, this one was not discovered by the Spanish conquistadors, but rather by an American historian in 1911. It is thought that the city was built around 1440 and inhabited until the Spanish conquest of Peru in 1532. However, there is no way to determine definitively exactly when it was built or who built it. Like other mysterious ruins from the past, it was built primarily of large stones; in this case, blocks of granite cut to fit perfectly together without mortar . . . so perfectly, in fact, that a thin knife blade cannot be passed between the stones.

The Incas used tools composed of stone and bronze. They possessed neither horse nor wheeled vehicle. Yet, somehow, these ancient peoples managed to cut and carry hundreds of these multi-ton stone blocks up the mountainside to a height of 7710 feet. Above 10,000 feet, World War II pilots and crews in un-pressurized aircraft required oxygen masks in order to breathe, but just 2000 feet below this critical atmospheric level, the Inca were somehow able to construct an entire city complete with running water.

It is not so much the how or the when, but the why, that intrigues me. Despite its lofty location, Machu Picchu doesn't appear to have been built as a fort, but rather as some sort of resort, complete with fountains. The builders integrated the architecture into the landscape. Existing stone formations were used in the construction of the buildings; sculptures were carved into the rock and water flows through stone channels. They (whomever they were) used advanced terracing and irrigation methods to cultivate crops. This is an extraordinary dedication of time and material to the precise construction of a city without any apparent strategic or economic value. It is almost as if this place was built as a work of art for purely aesthetic reasons.

Machu Picchu is not, however, the highest nor oldest city of the ancients. There is an older city, Caral, located 115 miles north of Lima, Peru, that is situated at an altitude of 11,500 feet. Thought to be the oldest city in the Americas, archaeologists have discovered a system of writing consisting of knots and multi-colored strings that was used at this site some 5,000 years ago. Their existence points to a sophisticated society where information on production, taxes and debts was recorded. Pyramid shaped public buildings were being constructed at Caral before the Great Pyramid of Giza was thought to have been built. What this tells us is that civilization was developing here more or less simultaneously with that in Africa and Asia.

In August 2005, archaeologists reported finding in Bulgaria 15,000 tiny golden pieces that are estimated to be between 4100 and 4200 years old. This treasure consisted of miniature golden rings, some so finely crafted, that the point where the ring is welded is invisible with an ordinary microscope.

Please note the similarity between the construction of the Mayan pyramid at Chichen Itza (next page) and that of the Egyptian pyramids at Giza (page 48). The stones are smaller, there are no casing stones, and, of course, it is much smaller, but the stone block construction is much the same. Other similarities include the four-sided design and the mathematical and astronomical precision. The close up photograph includes a picture of an orb "sitting" on the steps above (see arrow).

I have included a photo taken at the ancient city site of Luxor on page 65, not to show the statue, but to show the numerous "orbs" that hover about.

2. Pyramid at Chichen Itza in Mexico

(Please note the "orb" sitting on the pyramid steps.)

Orbs are mysterious transparent objects of unknown origin that were not discovered until the development of the digital camera. Since then hundreds of thousands of these things have been photographed (I find that I get the best pictures of them on a camera setting of 8 megapixels). Invisible to the naked eye, they are photographed most often in such places as old battlefields and ancient historic sites, although apparently they are everywhere.

3. Orbs surround this statue in the city of Luxor in Egypt.

CHAPTER 7 - UNIDENTIFIED FLYING OBJECTS

Since the very beginning of recorded history there have been reports of mysterious flying objects in our skies. There are even pictures of what appear to be alien craft in ancient caves once inhabited by our distant ancestors. Some of the paintings from the renaissance period include strange objects in the sky, albeit somewhat concealed in the background. The Aztecs, Incas and Mayan cultures include drawings and rock carvings of what appear to be some sort of flying craft. And, of course, I have already mentioned the numerous references contained within the Bible. It seems that every culture, every generation has been witness to these strange flying objects.

On July 20, 1945 in the desert in New Mexico, the first atomic bomb ever exploded on this planet was successfully tested. Two years later, unidentified flying objects (UFO) began flooding our skies, beginning with Kenneth Arnold's famous sighting. His description subsequently tagged these objects with the term "flying saucers" even though these objects have been observed in many different shapes since.

UFOs did not "burst" onto the national scene, however, until the sensational news story of a reported crash of a flying saucer that was recovered by the US Air Force at Roswell New Mexico in July of 1947. It was reported that alien bodies had been recovered as well. If true, the incident

67

was later "covered up" by the Air Force with "corrections," and, the cover-up continues to this day.

I will not bore my reader by recounting numerous examples of the thousands of reported sightings of UFOs and encounters with alien beings. There have been dozens of books and hundreds of news articles, even feature films, on this subject. I will only attempt to sum up with a few examples the highlights of the UFO controversy and explain what I believe to be the facts. During my lifetime, I have personally known two people who have had the experience of sighting a UFO within the relatively short distance of less than a mile. It made such an impact on them that it fundamentally changed their outlook on life, stretching the boundaries of what they had always believed in. These persons had no reason to make this up and I am certain that no one could ever convince them that what they had seen was not real.

Discounting the hundreds of thousands of eyewitness accounts that may not be accurate, we are still left with thousands of film photographs, 8 mm movie films, digital photographs, and most recently, digital films. These pictures have not only been taken by the average Joe on the street, but by news reporters, military photographers, police officials, civilian and military pilots, and astronauts. Yet, skeptics continue to dismiss all this evidence with fantastic, ridiculous explanations of what these people "really" saw and what these pictures "really" show.

Why these experts are so quick to dismiss these things and why ordinary folks (the non-believers) are so quick to accept these "explanations" escapes me. If you remove the single, primary argument from the theory that UFO cannot possibly be real because life on other planets is too far away to reach us, there is no reason that UFOs cannot be as much a reality as any other thing that we observe with our eyes and our cameras. But let us suppose that the speed of light can be exceeded by physical objects, perhaps many times over by "bending" some law of physics that we do not yet understand. Then all of the evidence we have, including radar records, military and civilian aircraft encounters, photos and film, and thousands of written testimonials must indicate to any logical person that was we are observing is real rather than an optic illusion.

What really lends credibility to the skeptics is the Governments complicity with "the Cover Up." When the incident at Roswell first occurred, the lower ranked military officers on the scene at the time were apparently willing to report the event. However, cooler and, more importantly, high ranking heads prevailed and an obvious belated attempt was made to cover up and hide the incident from the general public.

At the time, there were probably many good reasons to do this, at least plausible reasons. It may have been that the military expected to reap some technological advantage from the captured spacecraft, but a more likely scenario is that they assumed that the public would somehow panic at the news that we were not the superior beings at the very top of God's creation list. An example of Big Brother knows best if ever there was one. After the first cover up, I think it became self-perpetuating, since once you have lied, you have to continue with the lie to maintain your image of integrity. Perhaps this is how it all began.

In any case, I am convinced, as are many others, that there is an official Government cover up of the entire UFO subject. I know this, not only based on deduction, but also on personal experience. While working for the Navy I had the opportunity to ask Navy pilots about encounters with UFOs and their answers were unwaveringly consistent. "We have been *ordered* not to talk about that subject." Not "they don't exist"; not "that's all bullshit"; but "we have been *ordered* not to talk about it."

Civilian pilots fare little better. They have to suffer through tedious reports and official ridicule; most do not bother to report sightings. I have a friend who has read official classified reports regarding UFOs and these reports include details and specifics regarding these crafts that refute the Government's official explanation that UFOs do not exist. Because he had personally observed a UFO and had apparently gotten the official run around, Jimmy Carter, when he was running for President promised (largely forgotten) that, if elected, he would get to the bottom of the UFO issue, find out what the Government knew, and release the information to the American public. As we all know, he was elected, but the UFO issue disappeared like the morning mist, another promise betrayed. Shame on you Jimmy Carter! You can send me your official excuse and apology if you like.

Among the thousands of reports, there are only a few that I will address in some detail because they, more than any others, are indicative of a huge Government cover-up of the UFO "problem" and, they do indeed consider it as a problem. There are dozens of books on this subject, if one cares to research this subject further, including an excellent recently published book, *UFOs* by Leslie Kean.

It has been said that the only way that some skeptics will ever believe in UFOs is if one actually lands on the White House lawn. Well, this epic event almost happened. On the evenings of 19-20 July 1952 and again on July 26-27, the skies over Washington DC were repeatedly "violated" by numerous unidentified flying objects. On the evening of 19 July, seven unknown objects were observed on Washington National Airport radar that were not following established flight paths. These objects eventually flew directly over the White House and Capitol Building; both restricted air space. Sometime later, brightly lit objects that were traveling at an "unbelievable speed" were sighted by an airman at Andrews Air Force Base, ten miles from National Airport, while at National itself, a DC-4 pilot waiting to take off, observed six "white, tailless, fast-moving lights" over a 14 minute period. Later these objects were being tracked by radars at both

Andrews and National. At 3:00 a.m., shortly before two jet fighters arrived on the scene from nearby Newcastle AFB in Delaware, all of the objects vanished. After the jets ran low on fuel and had to return to base, however, the objects returned. Only about sunrise did these objects leave the area completely. These sightings made front-line headlines in newspapers around the country. Of course, then there was no CNN, FOX News, CNBC, or the Daily Show with Jon Stewart to report, in detail, these events.

Then, at 8:15 p.m. on July 26, a pilot and stewardess on a National Airlines flight into Washington observed some strange objects above their plane. These objects were soon being tracked by both the Andrews AFB and National Airports radars, and a master sergeant at Andrews visually observed them as well. Meanwhile, Albert Chop, the press spokesperson for the official Government investigation (Project Blue Book) into UFOs, refused reporters requests to photograph the radar screens. By 9:30, the radar center at National was picking up unknown objects in every sector and their speed varied between very slow and an estimated 7,000 miles per hour. Two fighters arrived from Newcastle AFB around 11:30 pm and they were ultimately surrounded and chased by four glowing objects that later turned away and disappeared. Other, more clearly defined objects were spotted by ground observers, including a "red cigar shaped object" spotted by an Army Artillery Officer over the Potomac River on July 19. He estimated it to be the size of a DC-7 and had a "series of lights very closely set together" on its sides.

His neighbor, an FBI agent, also saw this object. Eventually, this object moved over the city of Washington DC proper.

The radar contacts were later analyzed by radar experts and physicists who concluded that the targets were not "shapeless blobs as one gets from anomalous propagation ground returns," but solid objects and that the subsequent Air Forces explanation of "weather inversions" as the cause was virtually impossible. Still, the Government was sticking to their story.

All of these sightings made front page headlines across the country and details of the incident can easily be obtained by anyone who takes the time to "Google" them up.

Much more interesting and much more damning to the "anti-ufologist's" case that UFOs don't exist are the extensive classified records maintained by the US Government Military and, in particular, by NASA. These official records number in the thousands. Among the ones that we are aware of include the following:

On May 15, 1963, Major Gordon Cooper was on the final orbit of a 22-orbit Mercury mission (single man) around the Earth when he reported to the tracking station in Australia that he could see a glowing, greenish object ahead of him that was quickly approaching his capsule. The UFO apparently was solid and real because it was picked up by the tracking stations radar. Although this sighting was reported to NBC, reporters were not permitted to question Cooper after he landed. Major Cooper had earlier experienced a UFO sighting when he unsuccessfully pursued "metallic, saucer-shaped objects" in an F-86 over western Germany in 1951. They easily out-maneuvered his jet aircraft.

Later, in a taped interview with Major Cooper he was to say:

"For many years I have lived with a secret, in a secrecy imposed on all specialists in astronautics. I can now reveal that every day, in the USA, our radar instruments capture objects of form and composition unknown to us. And there are thousands of witness reports and a quantity of documents to prove this, but nobody wants to make them public."

Major Cooper also stated in another taped interview (with Ufologist Lee Spiegel) that he was aware of an official Air Force film that he had personally viewed "at least a dozen times," but after forwarding this film to Washington, the film "vanished"— never to surface again.

In June 1965, astronauts Ed White and James McDivitt were passing over Hawaii in a Gemini spacecraft when they saw a weird looking metallic object with long arms sticking out of it. McDivitt's pictures taken with a cine-camera have never been released. In December 1965, James Lovell and Frank Borman also sighted a UFO flying nearby their spacecraft.

Most "shocking" or interesting, depending on one's point of view, are the accounts of Neil Armstrong regarding the Apollo 11 moon landing. Armstrong and "Buzz" Aldrin are reported by various sources to have observed two "enormous" alien craft after landing on the Moon. This was relayed to NASA by Armstrong, but the tapes were censored and never released to the public. In fact, Aldrin took color film of the objects from inside and outside the lunar landing module, but these films have also never been released. Armstrong, who has confirmed this report, claims that the aliens, who have already established bases on the moon, "warned us away" in some unspecified, but clear, manner. The Apollo missions were subsequently cut short (by two missions) for "budget reasons" and we have not returned to the moon since.

The idea of alien bases on the moon is consistent with decades and dozens of observations of "strange lights" on the moon by professional and amateur astronomers alike.

There is no need to belabor the point with further detailed accounts. There are literally thousands of these from experienced astronauts, pilots, and other experienced, competent military personnel. Unless we assume that all of these qualified individuals are wrong, then the only logical explanation is that UFOs are real, they are flown by intelligent alien beings and the skeptics are wrong.

While some of the basic information described in her book has been previously reported, there are several interesting instances referred to in Leslie Kean's book, UFOS, that are especially significant in that they are important facts that have never before come to light, to my knowledge. In particular, she has expanded the coverage of a relatively well-known UFO incident that occurred at the RAF Bentwaters Woodbridge complex in England in the early morning of December 26, 1980. Shortly after midnight, three American Military security personnel; Sergeant James Penniston, Airman First Class Edward Cabansag, and Airman First Class John F. Burroughs went to investigate "some lights" in Rendlesham Forest just outside the base. What they found was a triangular craft about 9 feet long and about 6.5 feet high sitting in a clearing in the woods. All three security personnel immediately began having problems with their communication radios. Sergeant Penniston approached the craft that he described as having "blue and yellow lights swirling around the exterior as though part of the surface . . . like static electricity. . . but there was no sound from the craft . . . this was like no other aircraft that I'd ever seen before." The sergeant took close up photos of the craft and made notations in his notebook of strange symbols etched into the surface of the craft. And, then, and this is the most important part, Sergeant Penniston says "I just put my hand on the craft and it was warm to the touch. The surface was smooth, like glass, but it had the quality of metal, and I felt a constant low voltage running though my hand."

This is not just another case of "I saw something in the sky or even on the ground"; this is a case of "I put out my hand and touched it." No Venus, no swamp gas, no optical illusion here; this is a documented case with two witnesses of a military security person placing his hands on the vehicle.

About **forty-five** minutes later, the light from the craft intensified and it lifted off the ground without any noise and then shot off at an "unbelievable rate of speed."

Bear in mind, there are three trained military personnel within extremely close contact with this craft for at least forty-five minutes. Whatever this thing is, it is real and it is unlike anything these airmen have seen before (or since). The pictures (film) of the craft were taken to the base photo lab for processing. When Sergeant Penniston returned to follow up on the pictures, he was informed that none of the photographs came out: that they were either overexposed or "fogged." He was later advised to consider the entire incident as "Top Secret" and the matter disappeared along with the photos.

The problem with the "Great Government Cover-up" is, like all secrets, it is almost impossible to keep them hidden forever and the tide is running out on this one. Government officials in the know are getting on in age and their sworn to secrecy pledges are getting old as well. Apollo Astronauts are beginning to come forth with accounts of UFOs "escorting" them to the moon. Retired military personnel are beginning to tell of their encounters. There are stories of UFOs "shutting down" American nuclear missile silos for periods of time (including some rumors that this also happened in the USSR).

It is obvious that the aliens are interested in both our weapons and our space flight ability. I am sure that they consider both of these crude, but disturbing, especially the nuclear weapons. After all, they have so much invested in this biology project that they don't want us to ruin it.

Some countries are beginning to move in the direction of taking UFO's seriously and are releasing previously secret or classified information, including that held by the former USSR. The point is clear. The cover up is breaking up. As more and more credible witnesses, especially Government and military witnesses, come forward with revelations that have remained secret for years, there will come a time when not just the existence, but the substance and the extent of our knowledge of UFOs will become a matter of fact rather than speculation and the debate about these objects will cease. Meanwhile, the skeptical so-called "experts" will continue to swim upstream against the river of evidence to the contrary.

CHAPTER 8 - JESUS AND THE OTHER AMBASSADORS

If we go back to the Bible and look at the New Testament, which is primarily concerned with the life and teachings of Jesus, we see some strange similarities between what is written here and what is written in the Old Testament. There are also some significant differences. The main difference is that man is no longer speaking directly with God, but is now interacting exclusively with "angels" and "shining men" or strange men dressed all in white.

The similarities, however, begin right where the New Testament begins, with the account of the conception of Jesus according to Matthew.

"This is how the birth of Jesus Christ came about: His mother Mary was pledged to be married to Joseph, but before they came together, she was found to be with child through the Holy Spirit. Because Joseph her husband was a righteous man and did not want to expose her to public disgrace, he had in mind to divorce her quietly.

But after he had considered this, and angel of the Lord appeared to him

79

in a dream and said "Joseph, son of David, do not be afraid to take Mary home as your wife, because what is conceived in her is from the Holy Spirit. She will give birth to a son and you are to give the name Jesus."

Matthew 1: 18-21

Where have we heard this story before? There is no account of the birth of Jesus in Mark, but in the Gospel according to Luke, there is even a more detailed account of the so-called "immaculate conception." After an introduction that includes a similar conception story for John the Baptist, from the barren wife of a priest named Zechariah who was "well along in years," an "angel of the Lord" appears before Zechariah and tells him "your wife Elizabeth will bear you a son and you are to give him the name John." The Gospel of Luke continues:

" . . . God sent the angel Gabriel to Nazareth, a town in Galilee, to a virgin pledged to be married to a man named Joseph . . . The virgin's name was Mary. The angel went to her and said 'Greetings, you who are highly favored! The Lord is with thee.'

"Mary was greatly troubled at his words and wondered what kind of greeting this might be. But the angel said to her 'Do not be afraid, Mary, you have found favor with God. You will be with child and give birth to a son and you are to give him the name Jesus. He will be great and will be called the Son of the Most High."

Luke 1: 26-32

Soon after, St. Luke contradicts himself by saying that he "shall be called the Son of God."

"How shall this be," Mary asked the angel, since I am a virgin?" (Seeing I know not a man)

The angel answered "The Holy Spirit will come upon you, and the power of the Most High will overshadow you . . . .even Elizabeth your relative is going to have a child in her old age and she who was said to be

81

> *barren is in her sixth month. For*
> *nothing is impossible with God"*

> *Luke 1: 34-37*

This is an interesting passage because in it we have the Lord, the Holy Spirit, God, and most interesting of all, the "Most High." Even considering the fact that this account must have been written years after the death of Jesus and is based purely on here-say and speculation (with perhaps some embellishment by Luke, or whomever was the author), once again we have the same old pattern of events: miraculous births of sons to barren women and/or virgins predicted by angels of the Lord down to the naming of the child. God's fertility clinic must have been working overtime.

Neither of the gospels according to St. Mark or St. John refers to the conception or birth of Jesus. For more details of the birth of Jesus, we must return to the gospel according to St. Matthew. It appears that the famous three wise men were actually working for King Herod, who supposedly sent them to Bethlehem. Yet these wise men seem to have "appeared" from "the east" with the rumor of a "king" being born there and the rumor is what got Herod stirred up to begin with. It is at this point that the mysterious "star" appears in the east (from whence the wise men came) and they "followed it" into the east from where they had come "till it came and stood over where the young child was." Matthew 2:9. After these wise men are warned of (sic) *God* "in a dream not to go back to Herod, they returned to their own country by another route". Matthew 2:12. Sounds a bit more like a threat than a warning to me.

Once they had departed, the Angel of the Lord (not the Lord himself this time) appears to Joseph and warns him that he must take the child Jesus to Egypt in order to avoid being murdered by King Herod . . . .how could the "angel of the Lord" know this was about to happen?

Years later after Herod's death, a similar angel appears to Joseph and tells him it is now safe to bring the baby Jesus back to Israel . . . the why and the wherefore go unexplained. Thereafter, no mention of the young Jesus' life is included in the gospel according to St. Matthew. For that, we must return to St. Luke. But first I must digress.

In the version of Jesus' birth presented by St. Luke, there are neither wise men nor a "little star of Bethlehem" (my quotes). Instead what we have are shepherds keeping watch over their flock by night and "angels of the Lord" who come upon them, "and the glory of the Lord shone round about them; and they were sore afraid." St. Luke 2:9

What was this "glory of the Lord" that "shone round about them" and why were they afraid? Was it the lights (that shone round about them)? Could it have been electric lights that they had never seen before? Could this have been the "star" seen up close?

Furthermore, what is most interesting of all is that, in this passage of St. Luke, there are no angels of the Lord warning of Herod's eminent threat or besieging Joseph to flee to Egypt. There is only a reference in Luke 2:40 to "and the child grew, and waxed strong in spirit, filled with wisdom, and the grace of God was upon him."

Then there is the single final reference to Jesus' youth in St. Luke 2:45-49:

"And when they found him not, they turned back again to Jerusalem seeking him. And it come to pass that after three days they found him in the temple, sitting in the midst of the doctors, both hearing them, and asking them questions. And all that heard him were astonished at his understanding and answers. And when they saw him they were amazed; and his mother said unto him, Son, why hast thou thus dealt with us? Behold thy father and I have sought thee sorrowing.

And he said unto them. How is it that ye sought me? Wist ye not that I must be going about my father's business?"[5]

The same reference in "The International Version" of the Bible quotes Jesus as replying to his mother's question with the answer "Why were you searching for me? Didn't you know that I had to be in my father's house?" If these are the differences in today's versions of the Bible, how many differences have been made over the centuries and who did the final translations that we read today in English? Well, my guess is Catholic monks in monasteries. I cannot prove, but I can surmise that whenever the translation did not quite fit with the translators beliefs, that discreet changes were made to bring the story "more in line" with contemporary opinion of the religious leadership or the beliefs of the translator.

If Jesus truly existed, and there are those who have their doubts, then the question must be asked; what happed to him for those thirty missing years? What was he doing then? I believe that if Jesus were actually a product of a biological experiment between his earthy mother (the "virgin" Mary) and alien beings, then it is logical to expect that he was with "his father in heaven" as he so often refers, and that these beings were teaching him moral values that he would need later when he returned to "earth" to teach, heal the sick, and

---

[5] From the King James Bible

perform other miracles. I am sure that they would have provided him with the necessary tools to perform his "miracles" if this were the case. When Jesus appeared again at the approximate age of 30, he was on "a mission" to preach kindness and morality because that was he was sent to do.

Jesus never asked men to start a religion or to build churches based on his teachings. I believe that he was merely a good man/alien attempting to teach morality and kindness to one another as he himself had been taught. Only, much later, years after his death, did his following become a cult that, in time, became a religion. A religion that became twisted and was manipulated by later generations of "Godly men," many of whom were corrupt and used Christianity for truly evil, selfish purposes; never what Jesus himself had apparently intended. If he were alive today, I am sure that he would be saddened and distressed to see how badly his teachings were transformed and corrupted.

The alien's mistake, of course (a mistake that they would not later repeat in South America) was that, while they provided Jesus with the knowledge and means to do "miracles' and heal people (medicine), they did not provide him with any weapons. It is conceivable that Jesus may have become too enamored with his own "press" and believed that his alien "father" would protect him from all harm. If this was the alien's intention, they must have been "asleep at the wheel" when the Romans decided to crucify him. They didn't show up to save him and I think that he was genuinely surprised as indicated by his last words "My God, My God, why hast thou forsaken me?"

The aliens did not make this same mistake again. When they sent their ambassadors to South American to teach the Mayans and the Incas about science, agriculture, and morality, they sent with these men "powerful weapons" that struck fear into the hearts of those they taught.

However, following the crucifixion it is interesting to note that Jesus "arose from the dead" the next day after what is widely accepted as an "incredibly short" time to die from crucifixion (six hours). When "the women" went to the tomb, they found the tomb empty but were surprised when "suddenly two men in clothes that gleamed like lighting stood beside them." Once again we have "the shining ones" that seemingly appear out of nowhere. Could it be that the aliens did arrive "late to the party" but were somehow able to convey the appearance of death on Jesus and later return to revive and heal him? Is this when Jesus "ascended into heaven"? Did he ascend into "heaven" in a beam of light (as the aliens would have done)?

In Sylvia Brown's book The Mystical Life of Jesus, Sylvia writes that she believes Jesus survived his ordeal on the cross, recovered, and then escaped to Greece, Turkey, and eventually Europe. Then the apostles created the ascension into heaven story to cover up the fact that he had survived. I believe this to be purely speculative since there is no evidence to back this up or even to suggest it. However, her theory is, at least, more credible than Jesus rising into heaven in the traditional view held by many.

Putting it all together, the "angels", the missing 30 years, the miracles, the resurrection, the "angels" again, and finally the ascension story, steers me to the conclusion that Jesus, like others who came before and after him, were ambassadors for decency and morality sent by our creators, not divine creators, but creators none-the-less.

CHAPTER 9 - THE EGYPTIAN PARADOX

The strangest thing about the development of the Egyptian Empire, of course, is that it appeared out of nowhere, virtually overnight in the cultural time line. But the really huge paradox is why, in a continent otherwise exclusively populated by Negros, were the Egyptians of Caucasian lineage?

According to theories regarding the development of the different races, the Black man developed dark skin to protect him from the sun in tropical Africa, while the White man developed light skin because he had migrated to the northern climates where there was little sunlight and thus both no need for excess skin pigmentation. They needed sunlight for the body's production of vitamin D, an essential vitamin produced by the absorption of sunlight.

Yet, the Egyptians appear to have "evolved" with light skin in the intense sunlight of tropical Africa. There is no indication that they ever migrated from a northern climate and, yet, here they are a white enclave in a predominantly black continent. In fact, light skin was cherished by the Egyptian upper class who avoided exposure to the sun because "dark" skin was an obvious sign of someone who toiled in the sun, i.e. a common laborer or farmer. Suntans were not something special, but something to be shunned by the Egyptians. The facial features are also quite different with thin noses and lips. Most remarkably, this white Egyptian race changes radically to ethnically black Nubians at the southern border of the Empire; not a gradual change as one might expect, but a very abrupt change from white to black. How can this be explained?

CHAPTER 10 - THE GREEK PARADOX

The ancient Greeks were highly intelligent and were highly skilled in architecture, mathematics, writing (superior to the Egyptians). They were interested in astronomy and philosophy. They produced outstanding art objects and literature. In fact, Greek art and architecture were admired by the Romans so much that much of their works of art and architecture were inspired by and/or copied from the Greeks. Based on the hundreds of states that have survived from the classical era, it appears that the Greek people were of the Caucasian race and their eye color is reported to be predominately green or blue. They were an attractive people who put a premium on physical beauty. The faces on many of their statues have almost identical handsome features. Either the sculptors who chiseled these works were using some form of idealized model or the Greeks were uniformly attractive (see photo, page 79).

Their military organization and strategy, at the time, was the most advanced in the world (Alexander the Great later conquered most of known "civilized world" that includes what is now Turkey, the Middle East as far as India, and Egypt using tactics developed by the Greeks). The paradox here is that this highly advanced civilization with what appears to be composed of extraordinarily intelligent individuals had developed such a strangely immature religion or, at least, what appears to be an immature, even silly, religion. It was based on numerous individual beings with human like forms. Everyone should be familiar with the Greek Gods and Goddesses such as Zeus, Athena, Neptune, Hermes, and Mars . . . which were also copied by the Romans with slightly different names (Venus in place of Athena and so on). The Greeks had twelve Gods altogether, five of whom were male and, interestingly, seven of whom were female. The Greeks, at least, did not have a bias towards sex when it came to deities. There was no single God of either sex although the supreme Greek God Zeus was more powerful and more important than the others, a sort of leader of the group. These Greek Gods "lived" at the top of Mount Olympus "in the clouds" and "interfered" to some degree in the lives of the average Greek, or so it appears. Why would such an advanced culture develop such a complex, yet simplistic, form of religion unless there was some ancient basis for it?

The Greek legend for the beginnings of humankind was that "the creator" first created a class of people known as "the Golden Ones" who were exceptionally beautiful, lived lives of leisure, never aged, and died by going into a painless sleep. Doesn't this appear to be consistent with the alien biology project? In any case, it is both interesting and puzzling.

4. Taken in Corinth, Greece

The face with the lion's body fits the pattern of the sphinx, but what is with the wings?

.

CHAPTER 11 - THAT OLD TIME RELIGION

Christopher Hitchens has written an excellent book entitled *God is Not Great* in which he claims that religion poisons everything. In it he puts forth the case that religion, rather than being a catalyst for good, has become more of a springboard for all that is wrong with the human race – their prejudices, their intolerance for new ideas – especially those that conflict with what they, themselves believe in. In addition, it is invariably an excuse for imposing their will on others to the point that others are in danger of their very lives to oppose it. As a general rule, (and you can take this one to the bank), the more religious the individual, the more intolerant of anything that shakes his belief in what he/she is absolutely sure of – based on little more than the teaching of other equally intolerant men, who are certain that they, and they alone, are correct in their beliefs. This certainty is based in turn on nothing more than their teachings. The worst of the lot are those who profess to "know it is so because the bible tells me so," even from the mouths of those who have not even read the bible. They know the Bible only via what they have heard from the preacher's pulpit. A recent study conducted in 2010 indicated that those most ignorant regarding the actual contents of the Bible were the most religious while the most knowledgeable were atheist and agnostics.

In 2006, Christian Groups from various countries across the world, including Thailand, South Korea, India, and Australia were protesting the movie *The Da Vinci Code*, planning boycotts, a hunger strike, and attempts to block or shorten screenings. The reason: The film suggests that Jesus Christ was married to Mary Magdalene and that he fathered a child. When the Christian Church was at the height of its power in the 15th century, an idea such as this would have gotten someone burned at the stake. Even today, Christians become hysterical over any perceived threat to their way of thinking. What is it that they fear? Could it be the loss of our hearts and our minds to Christianity or their security of certainty? In the 15th century, it was the fear of the loss of the control of the church, a very real threat given the nature of the times and the mentality of the population. Can it be that even today Christians are so insecure in their belief that they feel compelled to put their finger in every crack of their ideological dike? Is the divinity of Christ that important of a component in their whole concept of self, morality and God that they cannot accept any other possibility without losing their conceptual bearings?

I think that most people believe in their own brand of religious philosophy based more on the fact that "everyone else believes, so it must be right," more than their own ultimate deduction based on well thought-out logic of their own creation. Religion makes it easy not to contemplate the ultimate question in life, i.e. what will happen when life comes to its inevitable end?

Carl Marx said that religion was the crutch of the people and I believe that he was right. There is a certain peace of mind that accompanies the certainty of life after death. But, the cold hard fact is that no one, not even those that say they do, has even a clue what will become of our souls once those machines we call our bodies simply wear out and die like my old Oldsmobile. So many people do not seem to know, or, at least care, that the Bible, both the old and the new testament are no more than legends written down by men and then translated from Hebrew, into Greek, into Latin, and then finally into French and English. Of course, each translator has put his individual spin on the writings, especially if what he reads does not agree with what he believes. It amazes me that a minister can take a small passage out of one of these books of legend and get a one or two-hour sermon interpreting it's "meaning."

Religion, in and of itself, would not be too bad if it were stated simply as "we were created by *something* who wishes us to live good lives for whatever reason" and others would allow you to believe in whatever you choose and not try to impose their beliefs on you. Unfortunately, this is not the case as so many Christians find the need to "save" your soul. Let them worry about their own souls and I will worry about mine. I hope that those born again Christians and their brethren who read this will take it to heart and leave the rest of us the hell alone.

Of all the religions, that I am familiar with, I know the most about Catholicism. This has to be one of the worst religions of all time. You can talk about how awful the Mayan and Inca sacrifices of human life were (and they were), but the Catholics were no better. During the period when Catholicism was at its peak of power, during a period still referred to as "the dark ages", over 100,000 women were burned at the stake for being witches, and hundreds of thousands of "infidels" and south American Indians were slaughtered in the name of religion during the Spanish conquest of Central and South America. A South American Indian's choice was simple . . . convert to Christianity or die; what would your choice have been? However, the most hideous of all crimes, in another way, was the destruction of thousands of ancient text and monuments of the South American empires that contained so much valuable historical knowledge.

Catholicism was developed by the ruling clergy with so many incredible rules and dictums that it boggles the modern mind; rules made by man in the name of God. They came up with two kinds of sin: venial (not too serious) and mortal (going to hell for sure). If you just were guilty of the venial sins you could "work these off" by spending some undetermined amount of time in a place called purgatory which, I suppose, was not as bad as hell, but still not pleasant; purgatory was something akin to a prison term.

They also decided that there was something called "original sin" that we are all born with, something to do with Adam and Eve. The purging of this original sin requires something called Baptism. If a baby died without being baptized, he/she would go to a place called "Limbo" which was neither heaven nor hell. The church has recently done away with this last piece of nonsense.

There is also the concept of the "Holy Trinity," i.e. the Father, the Son, and the Holy Ghost. The "Holy Ghost" thing has never been adequately explained to me and I have not a clue to this day what that is all about. And then you have confession, penance, Lent, the "stations of the cross", "holy" water, Ash Wednesday, fish on Friday (no longer practiced in reality), the "Virgin Mary", angels and, of course, Satin. The list goes on almost infinitely to the point of ad-nausea, but I will let it go at that.

There is no question regarding the existence of good and evil. I believe most of us understand these concepts and instinctively try to adhere to what is good; although our individual values tend to vary somewhat, in some cases, quite a bit. But to arbitrarily connect religious beliefs to morality is fundamentally wrong. There are millions of non-religious good people who do many good things, and, most disturbingly, there are millions of so-called God-fearing, religious folk who do despicable things . . . pedophile priests come immediately to mind. But Bible thumping TV ministers who prey on the gullible with requests for "prayer offerings" (received often from those who can least afford it) and other scoundrels who cheat, lie and steal go to church every Sunday.

For over two hundred years, the Catholic Church held the real power in Europe . . . during, once again, a period known as the dark ages. Excommunication was the big stick. If you were "excommunicated" by the church, then you were never going to go to heaven, and what could be worse than this during a period in which life on earth itself was hell? During this time, the Catholic Church murdered women for being witches or being under the influence of the Devil. Catholic Spaniards killed literally a million local tribesmen when they explored and ultimately controlled Central and South America. Progressive ideas, especially those ideas contradicting Catholic doctrine, were immediately crushed. Civilization in Europe actually regressed substantially during this period. Modern day Christians will brush these events aside with irrational excuses and stand firmly behind their belief that Christianity (and other religions, to a lesser degree, of course) is fundamentally a good institution. Good for whom, one might ask and for what good purpose do they serve?

No one knows exactly how much money is siphoned from the American economy each year by the various religious groups, but it must easily be in the billions of dollars; dollars from which no taxes are obtained for the general public good. Why isn't at least some of this money taxed? All of this money goes to church activities. The majority of the money is used to build huge elaborate buildings (we call them churches or, euphemistically, "houses of the Lord.") Sometimes the larger churches will even build special "retreat" camps and youth activity buildings. Only a token of the money obtained by most churches is used to help house or feed the poor, something that should be their number one priority, not the so-called "saving of souls" by preaching the gospel, often by ministers that are obscenely wealthy; paid for by tax-free money obtained from their congregation. Some churches even have advertising funds. As they are so fond of saying "what would Jesus do?" What would he think? Jesus never said, "Go forth and build large buildings in which to praise God." I believe that his message was to "treat each other well and take care of those that need help," as He himself helped them.

This is a direct quote from the December 22, 2010 issue of *USA Today*:

"The Roman Catholic Diocese of Phoenix stripped a major hospital of its affiliation with the church because of a surgery that ended a woman's pregnancy to save her life. Bishop Thomas Olmsted called the 2009 procedure an abortion and said St. Joseph's Hospital and Medical Center violated ethical and religious directives. St. Joseph's President Linda Hunt said the hospital could not "stand by and let someone die whose life we might be able to save."

St. Joseph's does not receive direct funding from the church. It will lose its Catholic endorsement, will no longer be able to celebrate Mass and must remove the Blessed Sacrament from its chapel."

"Violated ethical and religious directives?" What kind of ethical standard would place the unborn life of a fetus above the sanctity of a living person's life? The newspaper did not so state, but I assume that if this abortion was not performed that both the mother and unborn child may not have survived. Why can't this "church" understand this fundamental moral issue? I applaud the hospital's administrator's decision to disregard the ignorant church directive and proceed on what I consider the proper ethical and moral choice. This is just one example among millions in which religion has performed (or in this case unsuccessfully attempted to perform) an act that was detrimental to society or an individual, but was in accordance to their policy, a policy written by the unknowing and enforced by the unwitting. Again, religion and morality are not necessarily congruent. The difference between right and wrong are instinctively apparent to most people without the influence of religious doctrine. Morality is as personal a trait as one's taste in clothing and no one should pass judgment on the actions of others unless those actions adversely affect them.

Prostitution, a business transaction between persons in which both parties agree to an acceptable exchange, harms no one and yet it has been "criminalized" for centuries because the "community," usually the religious portion of it in particular, finds it offensive. I believe that the self-declared righteous crusaders should park their horses and limit their moral concerns to their own lives and those who share their beliefs and leave others to go their own way.

It is unfortunate that many have forgotten that "freedom of religion" includes the right not to have religion in your life at all, and the Government has never followed the "separation of church and state" principle since it has enacted many laws based on the not so subtle pressure of religious beliefs rather than exclusively for the public good. They have even placed "In God We Trust" on the face of our currency. If the Governments of these United States (local, state and federal) cannot avoid religious influence, how can we, the people, escape it?

Even good people will not obey bad laws because they recognize the basic difference between good and bad, right, and wrong. I believe that as we move into the future, a future filled with new exciting technology and great discoveries regarding life and the universe, that someday the majority of Earth's population will come to realize that religion is neither the answer to their uncertainty nor the arbitrator of right and wrong. The religions of the world in the end will, find themselves back where they all began, as relatively small cults of fanatical followers. There is statistic data that appears to confirm that this process is already well underway.

~

It took nearly six centuries to complete The Milan Cathedral (Italian: Duomo di Milano) in Milan, Italy, (next page) from 1386 until 1965. An estimate of its cost would easily be in the billions of dollars in today's money. This does not include the hundreds of thousands of hours of free labor contributed by volunteers in search of their ticket to heaven, very impressive, but very excessive.

5. The Milan Cathedral in Milan, Italy

6. St. Joseph Catholic Church, Jacksonville Florida

7. St. Joseph Catholic Church, Jacksonville Florida

The previous pictures illustrate examples of, in my opinion, exorbitant spending on the part of the Christian religions which is more for the glorification of the church than for that of God. This Catholic Church is only one of four large church buildings located on four separate corners of the same intersection. Some of the locals joking refer to it as "the four corners church." The buildings include the church itself, complete with fountains, gardens, and statues; an "Enrichment Center"; a parish with a school attached; and another large building whose purpose is not readily apparent. Next door to this mini-Vatican (complete with gold dome), there is a huge home for the Priest(s). The large tracts of land these building sit on are in an affluent area of Jacksonville and must have cost somewhere in the neighborhood of seven figures. This is for the land alone. Heaven only knows how much the church and the other structures cost.

The church's claim to "charity" fame is that they sponsor a food bank for the poor. In actuality, the food storage structure they use was paid for with a grant, it is supported by the entire community, the food is donated, and it is run by community volunteers.

I have included a picture of a huge, glass walled Protestant church for all of the protestant readers who are beginning to feel smug. Of course, there are thousands of similar churches in cities across America. Some defend this extravagant expenditure of billions of dollars by stating that the members of the congregation are paying the bill. In fact, everyone is paying the bill, church member and non-church member alike, because these churches pay no taxes on either the income they receive or the property that they own and that shortfall in taxes has to be made up by all of us. By being tax exempt the churches do not support public schools or departments of public safety, among others.

8. Protestant Church, Crossroad UMC, Jacksonville FL

According to the first amendment to the Constitution of the United States:

"Congress shall make no law respecting an establishment of religion, or prohibiting the free exercise thereof . . ."

However, nowhere does it say that this means that religious income and property shall be exempt from taxes. Taxing the church in America would greatly alleviate the tax burden on the rest of us by contributing to public services and may, in fact, be enough to enable us to reduce and/or eliminate our national debt provided the Government doesn't increase wasteful spending. But the sad fact is that no politician will take this issue on, or even talk about it.

CHAPTER 12 - PHYSICS AND OTHER FUN STUFF

Construction of the Great Pyramids and the city of Machu Picchu only seems remarkable when we visualize the enormous effort required to cut and move such huge quantities of stone with the assumed technical skills of people living during the assumed period of construction. Our logic tells us that, even today, using giant cranes and modern construction techniques, we would have difficulty building these structures. And yes, we would, because of something that we refer to as "gravity". Of the four known forces (strong nuclear, weak nuclear, electromagnetic, and gravity), gravity is the least understood. Although extremely weak on a small scale, gravity on the large scale is literally, what makes the world go round. Every object (mass) exerts an attraction to other matter, the larger the mass, the greater the attraction. In fact, contrary to common misconception, the moon does not revolve around the Earth; they both revolve around a common center of gravity. Gravity is such a fundamental force that it is the glue that holds the entire universe together . . . albeit when I say hold together, I actually am referring to conferring order out of potential chaos.

In its simplest form, the Sun and all its planets are a collection of balls of matter created by gravity sweeping up all the loose matter in their paths . . . like a large magnet passing through a pile of paperclips. The planets are revolving around the largest mass (hence largest gravity) in the solar system: the Sun. What prevents the Earth from falling onto the Sun, and the moon from falling onto the Earth, is velocity. The force of the speed of Earth as it revolves around the Sun exactly offsets the force of the gravity pulling us towards the Sun. If the Earth were to slow down, it would slowly spiral into the Sun, and if it were to speed up, it would fly off into space ("escape velocity" in NASA terminology.) Fortunately, for you and I, the Earth and the Sun are in orbital equilibrium, and have been so for the past 4.6 billion years; and we will be so for the next few billion years to come. During the formative years of the solar system matter, not in orbital equilibrium, either would have fallen into a solar system body (thus increasing that particular body's mass) or would have escaped into deep space.

The point of this exercise is to demonstrate that gravity, while it makes the world go round, is not all-powerful in the divine mechanics of the universe. We know that it can be overcome by velocity provided that the velocity can be sustained. We also know that the electromagnetic force can overcome gravity if there is a magnetic attraction between the materials being lifted. There have been some experiments where very small non-magnetic objects (such as a frog) have been levitated in an electro-magnetic environment; but to date, it requires a large amount of energy.

We are all familiar with the term "an object at rest tends to remain at rest and an object in motion tends to remain in motion." This is actually the short version of Newton's Law of Inertia that states, "Every body continues in its state of rest, or of uniform motion in a straight line, unless it is compelled to change that state by forces impressed thereon." The force applied to obtain the same results depends on the mass of that object, the greater the mass, the greater the resistance to a change of motion. Simply stated, it takes more force to move a bowling ball than a baseball, as it would take more force to stop it, given identical speeds.

Given Newton's Law of Inertia, therefore, an object such as a spacecraft should be able to continually increase its velocity indefinitely in the complete vacuum of interstellar space given the absence of any form of resistance, including any form of gravitational force, as long as there is a constant source of propellant energy. Light, on the other hand, leaves its source at its maximum velocity and retains this constant velocity as long as it does not encounter any form of resistance. This effect would be identical to a rifle bullet leaving the barrel of a gun at its maximum velocity of 2500 feet per second and continuing on in a vacuum indefinitely at that speed until it encounters some form of resistance. On earth, of course, that resistance is air and gravity and its speed quickly diminishes.

The one problem that a spacecraft would have traveling at or beyond the speed of light would be that any encounter with even a mass the size of a grain of sand would impart enough energy to catastrophically destroy the space craft.

This could be avoided, however, by sending ahead of the craft an anti-gravitational field to sweep the area into which the craft would follow clear of any tiny debris and dust.

Regarding the speed of light, one problem has always perplexed me. In January 2011, the Hubble Space Telescope found a galaxy that formed within 480 million years of the beginning of the universe when the so-called "Big Bang" occurred about 13.75 billion years ago. If the speed of light is finite at 5.9 trillion miles per year and we are looking back in time to where this galaxy was 13 billion years ago (the light just now having reached us), where is this galaxy now? If all of the galaxies in the universe are spreading away from the center of the Big Bang and the farthest we can see is 13 billion light years back, would we not be able to see only half of the universe; the half that is on our side of the Big Bang? And, if we can see galaxies on our side that are traveling in more or less the same direction as our half of the universe, how did we get so far apart so fast? This is just a thought. Let's shift gears to the mystery of gravity.

While it takes more energy to overcome a gravitational field for the heavier object, when two objects of different mass are dropped in a vacuum they will accelerate and fall to the ground at an identical speed. Therefore, the baseball and the bowling ball will fall at virtually the same rate (as will a sheet of paper and a sheet of iron given a vacuum). Newton believed that because small objects have smaller inertias than large objects that gravity must be applying varying degrees of force to overcome the size of the inertia of the object. From this idea, he obtained his Law of Universal Gravitation, which states, "Every particle in the universe attracts every other particle with a force that is directly proportional to the product of their masses and inversely proportional to the square of the distance between them."

Although this principle was accepted for the next 300 years, Einstein had a problem with it. He rejected the idea that gravity was a force that could reach out over great distances and pull an object towards earth with a power exactly equal to the inertial resistance of that object. Instead, he thought that gravity was a "field" similar to a magnetic field and he came up with something called the "Principle of Equivalence of Gravitation and Inertia." It states that there is no way to distinguish the motion produced by inertial forces from motion produced by gravitational force. To Einstein, bodies of mass do not "attract" one another, but rather gravitation is simply a part of inertia; that the movements of the stars and planets stem from their inherent inertia.

Einstein also postulated, since proven by observation that light passing through a gravitational "field" will be affected by that field and will bend inward toward the source of the gravitational field. Nevertheless, whether force or field, we know that gravity is a reality that constitutes a genuine force, which must be overcome whenever we attempt to lift or move something. It should also be noted that the magnetic field can function very well as a "force" when strings of electromagnets are arranged sequentially to reverse polarity along a track creating both levitation and great acceleration of vehicles moving on these tracks. This force is already being used today, with the help of modern computers, in amusement rides and will almost certainly be used some day in high-speed commuter and/or passenger rail service.

Despite Newton, Einstein, and the work of many others, we still don't completely understand gravity, why or how it works. But the fact that we can escape its grasp under certain circumstances teases us as soaring birds teased our great-great grandparents concerning the possibilities of heavier-than-air flight before we learned the principle of lift. One only has to assume that someday we will discover how to manipulate gravity as we manipulate electromagnetism, in order to make the construction of any stone structure a simple proposition.

It is almost a certainty that we will eventually learn how gravity works and how to negate and reverse its effects. Just because we don't understand it now, does not mean we will never do so. Our scientific knowledge is expanding at an exponential rate. We have learned more technology in the past twenty years than the previous forty and in the previous forty we had learned more than in the previous eighty. With the invention of the computer, whose power doubles every two years or so, we are on the very edge of huge breakthroughs in a number of scientific areas.

We know the aliens have already mastered the science of manipulating gravity because we have observed and filmed their craft hovering and moving about through our atmosphere without any visible means of locomotion or support, no rotor blades, no engine exhaust, and no engine noise. Somehow, they stay aloft and "fly" without using the principles of lift or thrust, the mainstays of our current flight technology.

If we were to drop a huge stone from a great height gravity would propel it towards the earth, rapidly accelerating at around 32.2 feet per second squared until either it smashes into a barrier such as the ground or it reaches the maximum speed allowed by the drag (friction) of the surrounding air; the so called "terminal velocity". For a human, this terminal velocity is about 120 miles per hour. Sadly, for the poor unfortunate skydiver whose parachute fails to open, a 120 mile per hour terminal velocity is more than enough to kill you; well, actually not the speed itself, but the abrupt stop.

If on the other hand, we could control the direction of the force applied by gravity and reverse its "polarity" from pull to push (like that of a magnet), an object containing such a "gravity reverser device" would theoretically accelerate upward at 32.2 feet per second squared continuously for as long as that object was within the limit of Earth's gravity (the so called "event horizon"). Once outside Earth's atmosphere, there would be nothing to impede this continuous acceleration. A trip to the moon would require reverse Earth gravity from here to the point where Earth and the Moon's gravitational fields negate each other and then reverse moon gravity to slow down for a moon landing. On the other hand, if this object was so directed, it could use the combined reversed gravitational force of both Earth and Moon to propel itself into deep space, although the force of gravity, and thus the acceleration, would decrease with distance traveled away from the gravitational source. The best part: while the craft is within the event horizon of the gravity source, the majority of the energy being used occurs naturally and the spacecraft would only be required to generate sufficient energy to direct the force of gravity. With a universe full of gravity points, range would be virtually unlimited. Of course, once in the vast regions between solar systems, it will take something more, perhaps the use of "dark energy," to make the jump to light speed and beyond.

On the other hand, it could be that only the small craft we observe from earth use an anti-gravity drive and that a large "mother ship" parked in solar orbit beyond our detection uses a more sophisticated engine to traverse between star systems. This goes a little against the grain of Einstein's theories, but, after all, we thought Newton was entirely correct for 300 years

The really heavy question, or "the long pole in the tent" as the military is so fond of saying, is the one always posed by the intellectual skeptic. "How could aliens visit Earth when space is so incredibly large and velocity is limited to the speed of light?" That is to say that since the nearest star is five light years away (186,000 miles per second x 31,536,000 seconds x 5 years or approximately 30 trillion miles), we are too far away from any other possible civilization for them to get here from there. In addition, it would take an unattainable amount of energy to move a large mass (such as a spacecraft) fast enough. You will hear this argument, I guarantee it, but this argument only works if you assume that the speed of light is the cosmic speed limit and you believe the claim that unobtainable amounts of energy are necessary to get there. Just because Einstein said it, does not necessarily make it so. In fact, there is some evidence and much speculation to the contrary. There is even some speculation now that the speed of light is not even a constant. Today scientists are seriously considering the possibility that the speed of light may be exceeded, not by forcing a material object through space, but by manipulating space so that it moves around the spacecraft at a rate faster than the speed of light. There are also theories regarding the bending of space and "worm holes" that create shortcuts through time and space.

The reality is that we don't know much at all about the mechanics of the universe. Each year, each month, each week we discover something new. Sometimes we still don't completely understand these things. We are in an exciting era. Changes in science are occurring every day. Major discoveries are a weekly event. With the advent of the computer, our scientific knowledge has been expanding at an incredible rate for the past 25 years.

When I was a child such things as quartz watches, microwave ovens, cell phones, lap-top computers, lasers, digital television, LEDs, GPS navigation systems, organ transplants, robotics, anti-viral drugs, cloning, and ATMs didn't exist. Only the most expensive automobiles had fuel injection. The average car did not have that, nor disk brakes, cruise control, electric windows or mirrors, seat belts, steel belted tires, air conditioning, leather upholstery, GPS, digital displays, CD players or even FM radio. These cars needed constant maintenance and wore out in about 100,000 miles. The average car today is quieter, safer, more comfortable, requires little maintenance, and will easily last 300,000 miles with proper care. All this has occurred in just my lifetime, a single generation. One can only imagine how far we will travel down the technological trail in the next 100 years and the 100 years after that. If we can travel so far so fast, how much more advanced must an alien race that has had 1000 or 10,000 or 100,000 years of technological head start on us? This is truly a wonderful time to be alive. We are just now emerging from the technological "dark ages" when we were literally ignorant of just about everything scientific.

What we don't know about physics is a thousand times what we do know. We now know that 96% of the universe is somehow "missing" but we don't know why or where. Because the universe is speeding up as it expands rather than slowing down (as expected) and galaxies are not flying apart as they should be based on the amount of visible mass, modern physicists now believe that most of our universe is not composed of matter that we can see, but "dark matter" whose additional gravitational forces are effecting us in ways that we cannot understand. In addition to this 21% of dark matter (real matter as we know it consists of only about 4 % of the universe), there is another 75% of "something" that is referred to as "dark energy." These dark parts of our universe must exert great influence on the way the matter we can see behaves and on the four forces that we know currently exist. Although no one yet knows how or why, someday we will, and in that day, in that time, WE will be the aliens traveling the galaxy, colonizing worlds and performing our own genetic engineering to create "civilized" creatures from the best raw animal material that we can find.

CHAPTER 13 – THE FINAL CHAPTER

CHAPTER 13 - THE FINAL CHAPTER

I could fill dozens of additional pages with facts and figures to further argue my point, but I believe the basic argument has been made. The facts are there, in hundreds of books and articles about the subjects that I have discussed in this one brief book. In my opinion, the theory set forth in these pages ties together the scientific principles of evolutionary thought with the numerous creation myths contained within various religious documents. I believe that someday soon there will be startling new discoveries in anthropology and archaeology that will definitely prove this thesis. I have absolute faith in it. The mystery of man's origin is relatively simple when compared to the question of the reason for the existence our species. Why do we exist? Why does life exist? Does the universe create life so that it can itself exist? Is all that we see and experience some sort of cosmic "game"? Is it the ultimate reality game, created and played only in something like the mind? Is that mental entity God? Does anyone really exist besides oneself or is it merely a perception?

If a living person were to lose each of his five senses (sight, hearing, touch, taste and smell), not as in a coma, but with an otherwise functioning body and brain, to the point that he/she existed in a total void, would that person still be "alive"? He/she would have no point of reference to establish his existence. Everything we know about life comes from feedback into the brain from those five senses. Take away one or two and the world still exists; take away them all and we exist only to those that can see or touch us.

Everything that we know about the world has been acquired by perception. We know that it exists because we have seen it, touched it, or smelled it. Our senses are limited to objects of a certain size, certain colors, or certain levels of sound. For example we cannot see infrared light and we cannot see microbes (thank God). Our brain struggles to comprehend the immensity of the universe. Like the housecat that spends its life confined within the four walls of its home, we are limited by our senses and our brain is limited to the four dimensions with which we are familiar. Furthermore, people, in general, are reluctant to contemplate such things as death and what lies beyond. They feel more comfortable believing that they know what happens after we die, although only those that have gone there could possibly know.

Our "real" living world is only what we can see around us. We cannot be certain what is beyond our ability to see and touch actually exists, but we are convinced it does in some cases because we have seen it before. We know that grocery store will be there when we go to find it

Heaven and hell may not exist, but the human mind perceives the existence of good and evil. Does evil exist so that good might exist? Does this make sense? Would life be meaningless or perhaps better if all existence were of the "good" kind? Would it all be too boring an existence for the human mind? These are questions of philosophy, not anthropology, but they are examples that illuminate the severe limitations of our brains to come to grips with the fundamentals issues of life that include our origins and our destinies. In the final analysis, we know not from where we come nor to where we go. We are only sharing a slice in the fabric of time with contemporary creatures with which we are familiar. Among those with whom we are not yet familiar, I am sure, are the alien species that have been visiting and manipulating our planet for hundreds of thousands of years. They are our true ancestors, our true creators, our fellow travelers in a universe yet to be explored.

If you cannot believe my theory, open the Bible to any page in the Old Testament and substitute the word "alien" for any reference to God, the Lord, or the Angel of the Lord, and you will see how the Bible is transformed into an informative book that makes logical sense. The ancient symbol of life for the Egyptians is in a modified version of a sperm cell; and there are pictures on some walls of what appear to be sperm cells. Without microscopes, how could the ancient Egyptians have known this? Could it really be just a coincidence? What happened to all the geniuses and where did they come from to begin with? Could all of the hundreds of thousands of documented UFOs sightings be wrong?

I invite the reader to look about them; read and listen, the evidence is everywhere. There are dozens of books on all of the subjects covered in this book and new scientific discoveries are happening every day that reinforce the idea that there really was a super race on Earth that did amazing things and created incredible things, including humankind itself.

I am confident that, in time, the theories that I have put forth in these pages will become evident to the point that they can no longer be readily dismissed. Every day that passes, every new technological development, every new anthropological discovery is bringing us one step closer to the explanation of our existence: that is, we are children of the caretakers of the cosmos . . .

BIBLIOGRAPHY

Archaeology, Barnes and Noble Books, 2003

Armstrong, Karen. A History of God. Alfred A. Knopf, 1994.

Asimov, Isaac. Of Time, Space, and Other Things. Avon Books, 1965.

—The Collapsing Universe. Simon and Schuster, 1977.

Barnett, Lincoln. The Universe and Dr. Einstein. The New American Library, 1957.

Binder, Otto. What We Really Know About Flying Saucers. Fawcett Publications, 1967.

Bowden, Hugh (Editor). Ancient Civilizations. Barnes and Noble Books, 2002.

Brown, Sylvia. The Mystical Life of Jesus. Penguin Group, 2006.

Calder, Nigel. Einstein's Universe. Viking Press, 1979.

Dawkins, Richard. The Greatest Show on Earth. Free Press, 2009.

Exploring the Unexplained. Time Books, 2006.

Greene, Brian. The Fabric of the Cosmos. Alfred A. Knopf, 2004.

Hancock, Graham. Fingerprints of the Gods. Three Rivers Press, 1995.

Hitchens, Christopher. God Is Not Great. Hachette Book Group, 2008.

Hynek, J. Allen. The UFO Experience. Ballantine Books, 1972.

John, Duncan. Astronomy. Paragon Publishing, 2006.

Kean, Leslie. UFOs. Harmony Books, 2010.

Kennedy, Roger G. Hidden Cities. Free Press, 1994.

Kirsch, Jonathan. God Against the Gods. Viking Compass, 2004.

Lorenzen, Corale. Flying Saucers. Signet Books, 1966.

Marrs, Jim. Alien Agenda. Harper Collins, 1998.

Mayr, Ernest. What Evolution Is. Basic Books, 2001.

Sagan, Carl. The Cosmic Connection. Dell Books, 1973.

Steiger, Brad. Alien Meetings. Ace Books, 1978.

Strieber, Whitley. Communion. Avon Books, 1988.

The Encyclopedia of Ancient Myths and Cultures, Quantum Publishing 2003.

Thomas, Gordon. The Jesus Conspiracy. Baker Books, 1997.

Tomas, Andrew. We Are Not the First. Bantam Books, 1973.

Tompkins, Peter. Mysteries of the Mexican Pyramids. Harper and Row, 1976.

—Secrets of The Great Pyramid. Harper and Row, 1971.

UFO and Alien Encounters. Alva Press, 2003.

Wells, Spencer. The Journey of Man. Princeton University Press, 2002.

TABLE OF FIGURES[6]

---

[6] All photos are by the Author.

ABOUT THE AUTHOR

Laurence Bergeron was born in Providence, Rhode Island but he spent much of his childhood living in Europe and Asia. After graduating from the American Academy in Athens, Greece, he attended the University of Georgia where he received a baccalaureate degree in economics. This was followed by a thirty-year Federal Government career with the Department of Commerce and the Department of Defense.

In 1997, the author received the Navy's highest civilian award, The Meritorious Civilian Service Medal for services that were of high value and benefit to the Navy. He is currently retired and living in Florida.

8845386R0

Made in the USA
Charleston, SC
19 July 2011